MARKET LEADER

Business Law

BUSINESS ENGLISH

Tricia Smith

Longman

FINANCIAL TIMES
World business newspaper.

Pearson Education Limited
Edinburgh Gate
Harlow
Essex CM20 2JE
England

First published 2000

ISBN 0 582 32842X

Set in 10.5/12.5pt Apolline, 10/12.5pt Meta

Printed in Spain by Mateu Cromo, S.A. Pinto, Madrid

www.market-leader.net

Acknowledgements

We are grateful to the following for permission to reproduce copyright material:

Financial Times Limited for adapted extracts from 'Resolution in a neutral forum' in FINANCIAL TIMES 21.4.1998; 'Court to hear key case on discrimination' in FINANCIAL TIMES 1.3.1999; 'Brussels files suit over bilateral aviation deals' in FINANCIAL TIMES 31.10.1998; 'Australian aborigines plan protests over uranium ruling' in FINANCIAL TIMES 23.8.1998; 'Bre-X minerals drama continues in the courts' in FINANCIAL TIMES 30.4.1998; 'BT launches fresh attack on phone crime' in FINANCIAL TIMES 6.7.1998; 'World banking system is a 'money launderers' dream' in FINANCIAL TIMES 25.5.1998; 'Inside the magic kingdom' in FINANCIAL TIMES 4.6.1999; 'Brit Biotech directors could face US lawsuits over marimastat claims' in FINANCIAL TIMES 3.5.1998; 'Ruling says where rot set in' in FINANCIAL TIMES 10.11.1998; 'Lego warns on change in law' in FINANCIAL TIMES 17.9.1998; ISCO for the extract from 'The letter of the law' by John Handley in CAREER SCOPE, Autumn 1997; National Consumers League for an extract from the article 'Cyberspace Fraud and Abuse' from www.fraud.org; News International Syndication for the articles 'Can Cannon be confused with canon?' from THE TIMES 10.10.98; 'Our bodies patently lack protection' by Edward Fennell in THE TIMES 15.12.98 © Times Newspapers 1998 and The Butterworths Division of Reed Elsevier (UK) Limited for an extract from PUBLISHING AGREEMENTS 5th Edition by Clarke, Palmer & Owen.

Illustration acknowledgements

Nick Baker for 5, 34, 58; Katherine Walker for 38.

Photo acknowledgements

We are grateful to the following for their permission to reproduce copyright photographs:

Associated press for page 47 and Rex Features for page 73.

Designed by Gemini Design

Project Managed by Chris Hartley

Contents

Arbitration

Before you read

Discuss these questions.

1 Have you ever been in dispute with another person over an agreement or a contract? What was the problem?

2 What steps can you take, apart from going to court, to settle a commercial disagreement?

Reading tasks

A Understanding main points

Read the text on the opposite page about how international disputes between companies are resolved and answer these questions.

1 Why might you prefer not to go to court in the country of your business partner?

2 What are the three main business areas which have traditionally been resolved by arbitration?

3 How is a forum made up for a neutral arbitration?

4 What is the main difference between arbitration and litigation, according to the text?

5 Which are the main arbitration centres?

6 In which city would you choose to arbitrate an east–west trading dispute?

7 Which specific aspects of a contract are named in the text?

8 What do clients look for from an arbitration service?

9 What examples of expert witnesses are given in the text?

10 Do all the venues share the same arbitration rules?

B Understanding details

Mark these statements T (true) or F (false) according to the information in the text. Find the part of the text that gives the correct information.

1 Disputes only arise in commercial transactions.

2 Commodities are things traders buy and sell, usually raw materials, like coffee, wool or copper.

3 A neutral forum has a balanced composition to ensure fairness to both parties.

4 New York is the only American arbitration venue named in the text.

5 Arbitration is a business in itself, for lawyers and their associates.

6 *Name recognition* for arbitration is like *brand awareness* for consumer goods.

7 International business depends on rapid resolution of contractual disagreements.

8 The courts of law in each country are less powerful than arbitration panels.

BUSINESS AND THE LAW DISPUTES

Resolution in a neutral forum

Arbitration settles international commercial cases, says **Jeremy Winter**

I DON'T THINK IT'S QUITE THE ADJUDICATION THEY EXPECTED EITHER...

You have been in a conference room in your lawyer's office for the whole day, negotiating a crucial international contract. Term by term, detail by detail, the lawyers have argued it out. Someone says: 'What are we going to put in for dispute resolution?' When you started the negotiations you thought that the deal was a certain money-spinner for both parties, so no disputes could arise. Now you are not so sure. So what do you say? What do your lawyers advise? Ideally, you might want to be able to have recourse to the courts in your own country: the other party would probably like to do the same in its home country. Neither is acceptable to the other, for fear of home-team advantage or even local bias.

The answer is to opt for arbitration. This is not really a difficult decision, and that is why arbitration is the recognised way of resolving international commercial disputes. For at least a century, it has been the dominant force in dispute resolution in areas such as shipping, commodities and construction. You can opt for a neutral forum and have a panel of three arbitrators, one chosen by each party, and the third (the chairman) chosen either by the parties or the two party-appointed arbitrators. In addition, you can keep your disputes away from the public eye, because arbitration takes place in private, unlike litigation in the court.

The main centres for international arbitration are: Paris, London, Geneva, Stockholm, New York, Hong Kong and Singapore. Which is used depends on the background and businesses of the parties. Stockholm, for example, was always the place for arbitrating east–west trade disputes, London for shipping and commodities. Singapore looks set for a busy time in the coming months and years after the Asian financial crisis. These locations, and the arbitration centres and lawyers working there, compete intensely. Arbitration bodies try hard to get their standard arbitration clause put into people's contracts, so they have a captive market once disputes arise. They do this by publicising their activities and their rules.

What they are looking for is 'name recognition'. In Europe, Paris (home of the International Chamber of Commerce and its rules) probably has the best name recognition, followed by London (home of the London Court of International Arbitration), and Geneva. What people look for in an arbitration is speed, cost effectiveness, confidentiality and reliability of the arbitrators and hence their decisions.

The choice of venue involves a complex balancing of a number of factors:

– the availability of good experienced arbitrators

– the availability of good experienced arbitration lawyers, and expert witnesses such as accountants and engineers

– the cost of these people

– the support or otherwise that the local legal system gives to arbitration. (For example, if the arbitration gets bogged down as a result of delaying tactics by one party, what powers does the arbitrator, or court, have to speed things up? Will the courts readily interfere or overturn arbitrators' decisions?)

– accessibility – basic things like flight access, good facilities (some of the best are now in the Gulf states), administrative back-up, good telecommunications, IT support and even climate.

National legislation also has to lend its support to such an important economic activity as arbitration. England has taken steps to improve English arbitration law in the form of the Arbitration Act 1996, which came into force at the beginning of 1997.

FINANCIAL TIMES
World business newspaper.

Vocabulary tasks

A Definitions

Match these terms with their definitions.

1	dispute resolution (line 8)	a)	unfair treatment
2	a money-spinner (line 11)	b)	accelerate
3	have recourse to the courts (line 16)	c)	reverse something already decided
4	home-team advantage (line 21)	d)	settling disagreements
5	local bias (line 22)	e)	make use of the legal system
6	financial crisis (line 55)	f)	benefit from being local or on home ground
7	delaying tactics (line 93)	g)	meddle or get involved with
8	speed things up (line 95)	h)	something that makes profits for everyone
9	interfere (line 97)	i)	ways of making things take a long time
10	overturn decisions (line 97)	j)	become operational
11	take steps (line 108)	k)	serious money problems
12	come into force (line 111)	l)	institute action

B Terms of disagreement and dispute

Use an appropriate word or phrase from the box to complete each sentence.

> resolve resolution dispute settle arbitrate
> arbitration arbitrator agree disagree delaying tactics

1 There is a serious problem we must try to ....*resolve*........ .

2 He was a distinguished lawyer who was an expert ....

3 The .... process took far longer than the parties had expected.

4 This was due to the .... employed by one of the companies involved.

5 The question is: how are we going to .... this dilemma?

6 When the goods arrived in poor condition, a .... arose over whose fault this was, and who should bear the cost.

7 The best way is not to go to court, which is public and costly, but to .... an agreement.

8 I believe you are wrong on that point – we .... on the interpretation.

9 There is always an answer if you try hard to find it: every difficulty has a ....

10 You cannot assume he will .... to those terms: you must check with him first.

C Parties to an agreement

In law, it is important to distinguish between the parties involved in a transaction or an action. Complete the sentences below, using words from the box. Not all the words will be needed.

```
signatories   buyer/seller   borrower/lender   supplier/producer   wholesalers/retailers
lawyer/client   teacher/student   plaintiff/defendant   licensee/licensor
franchiser/franchisees   undersigned   parties to the agreement
```

1 Everyone promises to obey the treaty – all major countries are ..*signatories*.. to it.

2 In the civil case, the .... brought an action against the .... for damaging his car on purpose.

3 The price was negotiated between the .... and the .... of the house, in a private sale.

4 The bank agreed that the .... should pay 12% on the loan, so the .... made a fair profit!

5 Manufacturers sell their goods to ...., and in turn, ... buy from them.

6 The relationship between a .... and .... is bound by confidentiality.

7 The beer can be produced under licence but the .... must fulfil all the requirements imposed by the ....

8 Some clothes companies sell their products on a franchise basis: each country has a main ...., with numerous people working as ....

9 A letter was sent to the manager complaining about working conditions. All the members wrote their names. The letter read: 'We, the ...., strongly protest about conditions at work.'

10 Many projects require the cooperation of various partners. If they all agree to work together, they become ....

D Word families

Complete the chart.

verb	person	thing
arbitrate	1 ..*arbitrator*...	2 ....
license	3	4 ....
5	6	franchise

Over to you

1 Recently there was a case of a mail-order company selling televisions over the Internet where the price of a top-line television was shown as $3 instead of $300. The web page was seen in many countries and several customers placed orders for the 'cheap TV', but the company said they had no obligation to supply as the price was a mistake. What do you think? Should the company honour the orders? Was it a contract? If it was, where was it made – in the country of origin or where the customer lives and ordered the goods? Is this a case for arbitration?

Discrimination

Discuss these questions.

1 Employment discrimination can be based on age, gender and race – are there other categories you can think of?

2 Are women and men employed as equals in your country, in terms of pay and conditions?

A Understanding main points

Read the text on the opposite page about an important case about discrimination against women in the workplace and answer these questions.

1 What is the case about?

2 Where is the case being heard?

3 Who brought the appeal – the ADA or Ms Kolstad?

4 What types of discrimination are mentioned in the text?

5 Why did Ms Kolstad sue the ADA?

6 Was there any dispute about the facts of the discrimination against Ms Kolstad?

7 What was the lower Appeals Court's decision?

8 Which organisation is mentioned that supports the ADA?

9 If the Supreme Court decides in favour of Ms Kolstad, how much may she receive in damages?

B Understanding expressions

Choose the best explanation for each of these words or phrases from the text.

1 knock-on effect (line 16)
   a) blow to the body
   b) wider consequences ✓
   c) entry requirement

2 malice (line 32)
   a) friendliness
   b) with bad or cruel intention
   c) unintentional

3 reckless indifference (line 32)
   a) driving without care
   b) heartless and cruel
   c) not caring about the consequences

4 upholds (line 47)
   a) reverses
   b) agrees with and supports
   c) sets a standard

5 brief (line 71)
   a) short letter
   b) legal document
   c) kind of case

6 caps (line 85)
   a) sets an upper limit
   b) interferes
   c) is the head

Court to hear key case on discrimination

By Patti Waldmeir
in Washington

The US Supreme Court today hears a case which could have a big impact on the size of damages paid by US employers in employ-[5]ment discrimination lawsuits. The court agreed to hear the case, Carole Kolstad vs[1] the American Dental Association (ADA), to clarify what kind of employer conduct [10]will give rise to punitive damages – damages awarded to punish and deter an offender – in lawsuits involving sex discrimination. However, law employment experts [15]said that the suit was also likely to have a knock-on effect on race, age and other employment discrimination suits brought under Title VII of the 1991 Civil Rights Act.

[20] The case involves a female lawyer employed as a lobbyist for the ADA, a professional trade association. A jury found that Ms Kolstad was denied promotion [25]because of intentional sex discrimination. The issue before the court is not whether this is so, but whether such discrimination must be 'egregious'[2] before punitive [30]damages are awarded.

Title VII permits such damages where there was 'malice or ... reckless indifference to the federally protected rights of an individual'.

[35]But in Ms Kolstad's case an Appeals Court found that the ADA's conduct was neither 'egregious' nor 'truly outrageous' enough to merit punitive damages. [40] At the moment there is confusion over the standard of conduct necessary to attract punitive damages, with the various circuit courts applying differing stan-[45]dards to define 'reckless indifference'. If the Supreme Court upholds the Appeals Court's decision in Kolstad – that the conduct did not meet this standard of [50]'egregious' – this would set a new standard nationwide that could limit the size of both jury awards and pre-trial settlements.

'Our concern is that punitive damages would become the norm'

Conversely, if Ms Kolstad wins, [55]jury awards and settlements could shoot up. Her lawyers argue in their brief that 'egregious' is too high a standard, and that employees need only show that their [60]employers knew or should have known their conduct was probably unlawful in order to have claims for punitive damages put before a jury.

[65] 'If adopted, this standard would subject employers to punitive damages virtually every time an employee engages in intentional discrimination against another,' [70]the US Chamber of Commerce argues in a brief filed to support the ADA. 'Our concern is that punitive damages would become the norm, not the exception, [75]whereas the law clearly intends them to be the exception,' says Stephen Bokat of the National Chamber Litigation Center, which has also backed the ADA.

[80] According to Jury Verdict Research, which tracks jury awards, 40% of verdicts in gender discrimination cases in the last six years have included punitive dam-[85]ages. The law caps damages at $50,000–$300,000 per plaintiff, depending on the size of the employer.

A lower court jury awarded Ms [90]Kolstad back pay after a male employee in the same office was, according to her lawyer's brief, 'preselected' for a promotion for which he was less qualified than she was.

FINANCIAL TIMES
World business newspaper.

---

1 an abbreviation for versus, meaning against

2 very bad indeed, disgraceful (widely used in legal terminology in American English)

Legal brief

Discrimination is unfair treatment or denial of normal privileges to people because of their race, age, sex, nationality or religion. In this case, the US appeal judges were asked to decide if the unfair treatment had been so bad as to warrant an extremely stiff penalty (punitive damages), which should deter others from similar behaviour. Note that each US state administers its own justice system but the system of appeal is from trial court to Appeals Court and then the Supreme Court, which is the highest appeal court in the US.

Vocabulary tasks

A Complete the sentence

Use an appropriate word or phrase from the box to complete each sentence.

> limit punitive damages egregious circuit judge Act settlement
> jury lawsuit brief cap appeal federal rights

1 The amount of money awarded to a victim has a ......*limit*......... .

2 The courts are in session at different times during the year in different places, so that the .... can work in a variety of places.

3 When Parliament votes to pass a Bill it becomes an ....

4 There is no .... on the liability of owners in a private partnership.

5 Many people think there should be a specialist .... for complex fraud cases.

6 American citizens should study their .... so that they know what laws protect them from abuse.

7 Damages set very high in order to deter others are called ....

8 A special term for very bad behaviour in the US is .... behaviour.

9 Every court decision may be sent for .... if circumstances justify it.

10 An out-of-court .... is desirable if possible.

11 Anyone can bring a .... against someone else if they feel they have suffered a wrong that cannot be settled easily.

12 A barrister cannot work in a court without a .... from a solicitor.

B Opposites

Match the opposites.

1	lawful	a)	illegal
2	clarify	b)	female
3	legal	c)	unlawful
4	malice	d)	one-off
5	preselection	e)	confession
6	male	f)	confuse
7	punitive	g)	token
8	knock-on effect	h)	kind intentions
9	discriminate against	i)	fair job promotion procedures
10	denial	j)	act fairly

C Prepositions

Complete these sentences with a preposition from the box.

> up   under   against   on   to   at

1 If she wins this case, awards and settlements could shoot ......*up*........... .
2 The suits are brought .... Title VII of the 1991 Civil Rights Act.
3 There may be a knock- .... effect: other types of discrimination suits will be affected.
4 The decision will have a major impact .... employers nation-wide.
5 Some companies may be subject .... enormous claims.
6 The law caps damages .... a certain sum of money, depending .... the size of the company.
7 According .... the researchers, juries often award punitive damages in cases where there has been discrimination .... women in the workplace.
8 What kind of conduct could give rise .... punitive damages?

D Different outcomes

Use an appropriate word or phrase from the box to complete each sentence.

> however   on the other hand   if   whereas
> should   conversely   might

1 The court could decide to award punitive damages for any justified complaint. ....*However*...., if that happened, companies would soon go bankrupt.
2 On the one hand, the lower court may decide in favour of the plaintiff; ...., the appeal court may decide differently.
3 The verdict may be to limit all types of damages. ...., the verdict may be to award the maximum possible to deter others.
4 .... they had not complained about the award, there would not have been an appeal.
5 A successful outcome for the company involved would be a limitation on the damages, ... a worst-case scenario would be that they have to pay punitive damages.
6 .... the worst come to the worst, the ADA .... find themselves paying Ms Kolstad punitive damages – and others too, if they file suit!

Over to you

1 Check what the law in your country says about employment and equal opportunities. How do these affect disabled people? Write a brief report.

2 Research some advertisements on TV or in magazines. Can you find any which use thought-provoking or socially challenging images? List the kinds of discrimination the advertisements try to make the public aware of.

Competition

Before you read

Discuss these questions.

1 Does your country have a national airline? Does it have special privileges, like a subsidy or special airport facilities?

2 Do you travel by air frequently? What was the reason for your latest flight? Could you choose between several different airlines for the same trip?

3 Should all airlines be allowed to compete on fare prices, as other industries do?

4 Do you agree with free trade and competition, or is there a good reason to regulate some markets?

Reading tasks

A Understanding main points

Mark these statements T (true) or F (false) according to the information in the text on the opposite page. Find the part of the text that gives the correct information.

1 The European Commission is in Brussels.   T

2 An alliance is the same as a merger.

3 Washington and Brussels are holding discussions at the moment on an open skies policy.

4 *Open skies policy* means any airline can fly anywhere.

5 BA and American Airlines agree how much the fares should be on each other's flights.

B Understanding details

Answer these questions.

1 Which organisation is taking eight European countries to court?

2 Find the exact words that say what aspect of the law has been broken.

3 Why does the EU object to agreements between an individual European country and the US?

4 What does BA hope to do with American Airlines?

5 What does the Competition Commissioner do in the European Commission?

6 When does BA intend to conclude a code-sharing deal with American Airlines?

Brussels files suit over bilateral aviation deals

By Michael Smith in Brussels

The European Commission is taking eight European countries to the European Court of Justice over their bilateral aviation deals with the US. The EU's executive said yesterday that the deals distorted the EU air market to the detriment[1] of European carriers.

Disclosure of the move coincided with confirmation by British Airways (BA) that it was scaling back plans for a full alliance with American Airlines because of regulatory difficulties. BA is also pressing the British government to reach an agreement with the US for a gradual liberalisation of the US air market. Talks between Brussels and Washington on a full open skies policy broke down last month.

The European Commission's decision to file suit against the UK, Austria, Belgium, Denmark, Finland, Germany, Luxembourg and Sweden follows a long campaign to win the approval of EU member states for seeking an EU-wide deal with the US. 'There need be no roll-back,' the Commission said. 'These individual agreements can be written into a wider deal.'

The European Transport Commissioner said member states created serious competition distortions by unilaterally granting US carriers rights while ensuring exclusivity for their own carriers. EU rules were rendered ineffective[2] by the deals, he said. The Commission warned member states four years ago that bilateral deals with the US would be illegal and would jeopardise[3] the creation of an EU-wide deal with Washington.

Most of the bilateral agreements have been signed since then. However, the Commission held off taking legal action after winning approval from member states for starting 'open sky' talks. It re-activated legal proceedings after EU countries last spring rejected its request for widening the scope of the talks to include market access and traffic rights – the rights to fly to and inside another country's territory – and will not negotiate a deal unless the terms are widened.

In London, BA said it was still committed to getting a full deal with American Airlines in the long run. 'We want an alliance with American because the customer now thinks and travels globally,' it said. 'But the terms put forward by the European Competition Commissioner are not acceptable to us commercially.'

The Competition Commissioner has demanded that BA and American should give up 267 weekly slots free of charge at London's Heathrow and Gatwick airports. In the transition period towards full liberalisation, BA plans to conclude a code-sharing agreement with American. This would allow them to sell seats on each other's flights, but they would not set fares jointly.

FINANCIAL TIMES
World business newspaper.

1 disadvantage

2 made useless

3 put at risk

C How the text is organised

What do these underlined words refer to in the text?

1 disclosure of the <u>move</u> (line 9)   *taking eight European countries to court*

2 <u>it</u> was scaling back plans (line 11)

3 <u>These</u> individual agreements (line 31)

4 <u>their</u> own carriers (line 39)

5 <u>It</u> re-activated legal proceedings (line 54)

6 <u>its</u> request for widening the scope (line 56)

Legal brief

The purpose of the EU is to form a common market between members that is unrestricted by tariff barriers. In 1986, a Single Market Act proposed the removal of all trade barriers and tariffs by 1992. The European Commission works on behalf of the EU to make routine decisions and to propose new laws that will apply to all members. The Commissioner responsible for transport policy has disciplined eight EU member states for trying to make private deals with the US, rather than cooperating in the Common Aviation Policy.

Vocabulary tasks

A Understanding expressions

Choose the best explanation for each of these words and phrases from the text.

1 disclosure (line 9)
   a) telling the public
   b) keeping a secret
   c) ending a meeting

2 regulatory difficulties (line 13)
   a) problems with the authorities
   b) rivalry between competitors
   c) financial disputes

3 gradual liberalisation (line 17)
   a) rapid change of policy
   b) refusal to change policy
   c) slow relaxation of policy

4 roll-back (line 30)
   a) delay
   b) going back on present deals
   c) limiting the agreements

5 ensuring exclusivity (line 38)
   a) paying insurance
   b) offering deals to several parties
   c) guaranteeing a deal with only one partner

6 transition period (line 78)
   a) time of no change
   b) in the middle of change
   c) after change has finished

B Definitions

Match these terms with their definitions.

1 bilateral (line 4)
2 distort (line 6)
3 detriment (line 8)
4 file suit (line 23)
5 unilateral (line 37)
6 rendered ineffective (line 40)
7 held off (line 51)
8 widen the scope (line 56)

a) go to court
b) two sides
c) extend the limits
d) negative effect
e) made useless
f) changed, in a bad way
g) waited to act
h) done by one person or company

C Competition words

Use an appropriate word or phrase from the box to complete each sentence.

> monopoly   competition   regulation   regulated   deregulated
> free trade   unfair competition   protectionism

1 Tobacco can only be sold at state shops in Spain: it is a ..*monopoly*.....

2 When two or more companies want to sell their goods to the same customers, they are in .... with each other.

3 It is .... when the rules of business do not apply equally to all participants.

4 When the European Commission issues rules about how firms do business, the market is said to be ....

5 When those rules are removed and the market is free, the market is said to be ....

6 .... is the concept of doing international business with no barriers or restrictions.

7 If one country tries to keep out foreign competitors so that national industries will be safe, it is called ....

8 The concept of .... is that of ordering and controlling how business is conducted.

Over to you

1 Are there any protected industries in your country? Why do you think these industries are protected? Are there any advantages in keeping out competitors? Make a list of points for and against the regulation of competition.

2 You have decided to start a sports shoe retail business. Are you going to sell locally-made shoes or import them from other countries at a lower price? Think of some legal factors you should consider when entering the market: for example, are there import taxes on foreign goods? What government protection for local industry is there?

Brand names

Discuss these questions.

1 'A rose by any other name would smell as sweet,' wrote William Shakespeare. Do you agree? How important and valuable are brand names?

2 In your country, are there many international brands? Do you know where the brands originate?

A Understanding main points

Read the text on the opposite page about a dispute between two international companies with very similar brand names and answer these questions.

1 What characteristics of a trademark must be taken into account in this dispute?

2 Which treaty does the case refer to?

3 What products are made by the two companies in the text?

4 Why did Canon oppose the German registration of Cannon?

5 Which company used the trademark first – the Japanese company (Canon) or the US one (MGM)?

6 Which two main questions did the court consider?

7 What is the essential function of a trademark?

8 What confusion must the public be protected against?

9 What kind of competition does the Treaty aim to establish?

10 Was MGM allowed to register its trademark *Cannon* in Germany? Who won the case?

B Understanding details

Answer these questions.

1 Why is *reputation* important for trademarks?

2 Why does the earlier trademark have a stronger claim than the later one?

3 What is included in the concept of *confusion* on the part of the public?

4 Why does the case law mention the distinctive nature of the trademark?

5 What exactly does a *single undertaking* refer to? (line 121)

6 Is it true that trademarks which are very distinctive have greater protection under the law than unmemorable or vague ones?

7 Does *undistorted* competition mean the same as *unfair* competition?

8 How does a trademark enable a consumer to distinguish between similar products or services?

European Law Report   Luxembourg

Can 'Cannon' be confused with 'Canon'?

Canon Kabushiki Kaisha vs Metro-Goldwyn-Meyer Inc

Case C-39/97

Before the Court of Justice of the European Communities in Luxembourg

[Judgment 29 September 1998]

The distinctive character of a trademark, in particular its reputation, had to be taken into account in determining whether there was sufficient similarity between the goods and services covered by that and another proposed mark to give rise to the likelihood of confusion.

The Court of Justice of the European Communities so held, inter alia[1], on a reference by the German Federal Court of Justice for a preliminary ruling under Article 177 of the EC Treaty re: Article 4(1)b of the Directive of 21 December 1988 relating to trademarks.

MGM applied in Germany for registration of the word trademark 'Cannon' to be used for video film cassettes and film production distribution and projection for cinemas and television.

Canon Kabushiki Kaisha opposed the application on the ground that it infringed its earlier world trademark 'Canon' registered in Germany in respect of, inter alia, still and motion picture cameras, and projectors, and television filming, recording, transmission, receiving and reproduction devices, including tape and disc devices.

In the course of the proceedings, it was held, inter alia, that the mark 'Canon' had a reputation, but no importance was to be attached to that fact in deciding whether the marks were relevantly similar.

Article 4(1) of Directive 89/104 provides:

'A trademark shall not be registered or, if registered, shall be liable to be declared invalid, if because of its identity with or similarity to, the earlier trademark and the identity or similarity of the goods or services covered by the trademarks, there exists a likelihood of confusion on the part of the public, which includes the likelihood of association with the earlier trademark.'

In its judgment the Court of Justice held:

The first question was whether the distinctive character of the earlier mark, and in particular its reputation, were to be taken into account in determining the issue of similarity.

Furthermore, according to the case law of the Court, the more distinctive the earlier mark, the greater the risk of confusion: since protection of a trademark depended, in accordance with Article 4(1)b of the Directive, on there being a likelihood of confusion; marks with a highly distinctive character, either per se[2] or because of the reputation they possessed on the market, enjoyed broader protection than marks with a less distinctive character.

It followed that, for the purposes of Article 4(1)b, registration of a trademark might have to be refused, despite a lesser degree of similarity between the goods and services covered, where the marks were very similar and the earlier mark, in particular its reputation, was highly distinctive.

The second question was whether there could be a likelihood of confusion within the meaning of Article 4(1)b where the public perception was that the goods or services had different places of origin. There was such likelihood of confusion where the public could be mistaken as to the origin of the goods or services.

The essential function of the trademark was to guarantee the identity of the origin of the marked product to the consumer or end user by enabling him, without any possibility of confusion, to distinguish the product or service from others which had another origin.

For the trademark to be able to fulfil its essential role in the system of undistorted competition which the Treaty sought to establish, it had to offer a guarantee that all the goods or services bearing it had originated under the control of a single undertaking which was responsible for their quality.

Accordingly, the risk that the public might believe that the goods or services in question came from the same undertaking or economically linked undertakings constituted a likelihood of confusion within the meaning of Article 4(1)b.

Consequently, in order to demonstrate that there was no likelihood of confusion, it was not sufficient to show simply that there was no likelihood of the public being confused as to the place of production of the goods or services.

On those grounds the Court of Justice ruled:

There could be likelihood of confusion within the meaning of Article 4(1)b even where the public perception was that the goods or services had different places of production. By contrast, there could be no such likelihood where it did not appear that the public could believe that goods or services came from the same undertaking or from economically linked undertakings.

1 among other things (Latin)

2 in itself (Latin)

From *The Times: Law Report*

Legal brief

In this case, the European Court of Justice ruled that the public could easily mistake Canon and Cannon as being the same company selling the same products and, therefore, did not allow Cannon to be registered as a legal brand name in Europe. Canon was the winner for having established its name and brand already in the market. In English law, where a trademark, label, logo or design is used to intentionally confuse the public into thinking that the product belongs to a well-known brand the crime is called 'passing off'.

Vocabulary tasks

A Collocations

Match these words as they occur in the text.

1	public	a)	of confusion
2	goods	b)	perception
3	world	c)	competition
4	course	d)	trademark
5	take	e)	or services
6	likelihood	f)	into account
7	undistorted	g)	of proceedings

B Complete the sentence

Use an appropriate phrase from Exercise A to complete each sentence.

1 _Public perception_. is what the court thinks people generally think.

2 The court has to .... the reputation of the trademark.

3 The judge held, during the ...., that the company was a monopoly.

4 What businesses do is to provide .... for consumers and customers.

5 In the case of similar trademarks, there is a strong ....

C Verbs of misleading

Use an appropriate word or phrase from the box to complete each sentence.

passing off   impersonate   copy   lead (someone) to think

1 _Passing off_... is a crime. It involves making a new product look like a well-established one.

2 The judge asked the prisoner what .... he deserved a lesser punishment.

3 The picture I have on my wall is only a .... of a Corot – I wish it were the real thing!

4 The dictator hired several men to .... him at official functions to confuse his enemies.

D Giving reasons and justifying decisions

Use an appropriate word or phrase from the box to complete each sentence.

> on the grounds   it was held   according to case law   for the purpose of
> proper construction   within the meaning of

1 The case was dismissed ..*on the grounds*.. of inadmissible evidence.

2 There are several views but ...., it must be seen that an infringement occurred.

3 The High Court reported that, ... the Article, there was no likelihood of confusion.

4 On a .... of Article 4(c) of the Directive, the distinctive nature of the trademark had to be demonstrated.

5 .... that only within a rather restricted understanding could there be confusion.

6 More evidence was needed .... clarifying exactly what happened.

E Prepositions

Complete these sentences with an appropriate preposition.

1 A similar trademark could give rise ....*to*......... the likelihood ....*of*......... confusion.

2 The name was registered .... respect ...., cameras and films.

3 The law depends .... the interpretation .... certain Articles.

4 *Canon* was originally registered .... Germany .... a Japanese company.

5 A trademark may be invalid because of its identification .... or similarity .... an earlier trademark.

6 The Federal Court .... Justice .... Germany asked .... a preliminary ruling .... Article 177 of the EC Treaty.

7 .... the meaning of the same Article, there was the second question relating .... the place .... origin.

8 The trademark should clearly guarantee that goods bearing it had originated .... the control .... a single company.

Over to you

1 Have you ever bought something which you thought was a branded item, or a famous make, only to discover it was a fake? What did you do? Does having the 'real' thing matter?

2 Write a letter to your local Consumers' Association complaining that in your local market there are numerous watches on sale that seem to be a famous brand but turn out to be fakes.

Patents and intellectual property

Discuss these questions.

1 What is a patent?

2 Are there laws in your country forbidding the cloning – making exact genetic copies – of humans?

3 Can you see any dangers in the 'ownership' of scientific knowledge? If a new medical breakthrough is made by a scientific team, should they be able to keep it to themselves until the price is right and profit from it?

Reading tasks

A Understanding main points

Mark these statements T (true) or F (false) according to the information in the text on the opposite page. Find the part of the text that gives the correct information.

1 Solicitors like very technical and specialised areas of law.   F

2 It is legal to clone humans for spare parts at present in the UK.

3 Patents protect the formulae of drugs for ever.

4 Patent law is well understood by most small research companies in the UK.

5 The most critical part of an Intellectual Property protection programme is a complete set of contractual documentation.

6 The inventiveness of scientists will have to be matched by the changes in the law.

B Understanding details

Answer these questions.

1 What were the *two events* referred to in line 5?

2 How many official bodies are named that deal with cloning and genetics? What are they?

3 What do the firms need to produce if they want complete IP protection?

4 What kind of effect should this report have on the small research-based companies?

5 What kind of discussions are there likely to be about making money out of scientific research?

6 What might larger companies do if they find a discovery is not patented?

7 Which phrase in the last paragraph means the same as *see only the tip of the iceberg?*

8 What kind of legal issues does the cloning debate cause?

Our bodies patently lack protection

Intellectual property needs proper safeguarding, says **Edward Fennell**

The marriage of intellectual property (IP) and life sciences creates one of those niche practices of law that most solicitors like to avoid. But two events recently brought home the importance of this area of law.

First, the recommendation by the UK Human Fertilisation and Embryology Authority to permit human cloning for 'spare parts' is likely to create a huge wave of research leading to a flood of patent registrations and subsequent litigation. Penny Gilbert, of the IP firm Bristows, says that though the European Commission Biotechnology Directive specifically excludes human cloning processes from patentability, it does not apply to such parts of the human body as tissue. 'There are', she says, 'potentially valuable patents in this field and litigation between rival researchers is almost inevitable.'

Elsewhere in the market, the pharmaceutical companies Zeneca and Astra were deep in talks about a merger. Both face the imminent end of the patent on several drugs, and need more resources to plug the gaps. Patents are probably these companies' most important single resource and the big pharmaceutical companies and life sciences firms jealously guard them. Larger law firms such as Cameron McKenna and Herbert Smith are often engaged in litigation to protect rights that may have been infringed.

Smaller research-based companies are not always so alert to the dangers and opportunities of patent law. A recent report, commissioned by Taylor Joynsen Garrett from the London Business School, says: 'There is evidence of a surprising lack of recognition of the importance of IP protection.' Almost a third of companies think their investors 'understand little' or 'not at all' the nature of their IP rights.

'Litigation between rival researchers is almost inevitable'

Only two-thirds of companies said that when it came to IP, due diligence[1] had been undertaken by their investors where it was relevant before financing their most recent investment.

Just over half the smaller companies have a programme in place to ensure that all IP rights produced by their research development are adequately protected. And many that have an IP protection programme do not produce a complete set of contractual documentation to cover dealings in IP rights, even though this is potentially the most critical component of all.

The report is a wake-up call to smaller research-based companies to take the legal implications of their work seriously. While there are bound to be ethical debates about the right to make money out of this kind of activity, there is no question that larger companies will have little hesitation in capitalising on discoveries not properly protected. Ms Gilbert believes that we are only starting to scratch the surface of developments in this field. How it turns out will be shaped as much by the application of the law as by the inventiveness of scientists. And though the Biotechnology Directive excludes human cloning processes from patentability, commercial companies will not stop doing the work, nor stop generating complex and puzzling legal issues.

1 the opposite of *negligence*; used by auditors and lawyers to show they have checked very carefully all the available documents in order to determine if a fact or figure is correct, or who is the current and legal owner of land, property or ideas

From *The Times*

Vocabulary tasks

A Definitions

Match these terms with their definitions.

1 proper safeguarding (title)		**a)**	complete set of details about IP rights dealings
2 niche practices (line 4)		**b)**	break a law or regulation
3 patent registration (line 14)		**c)**	adequate protection
4 patentability (line 20)		**d)**	begin to understand something
5 litigation (line 24)		**e)**	taking advantage of a commercial opportunity
6 infringe (line 42)		**f)**	application for the sole rights of ownership
7 due diligence (line 57)		**g)**	allowing an invention to be registered
8 contractual documentation (line 69)		**h)**	bringing a lawsuit against someone
9 capitalising (line 82)		**i)**	thorough investigation
10 scratch the surface (line 86)		**j)**	specialised areas of expertise

B Metaphors

Use an appropriate phrase from the box to complete each sentence.

> wave of research   flood of patent registrations   stop the leak   plug the gap
> scratch the surface   gone up in smoke   avalanche of complaints
> landmark case   cast a shadow over   dawned on

1 Permission from the European Courts to allow cloning will bring a .....*wave of research*.... which will lead to a .*flood of patent registrations*..

2 This problem is bigger than you think. We have only just begun to ....

3 Our rivals have copied our work. All our hopes have ....

4 The drug caused severe headaches and vomiting. There was an .... from doctors and patients.

5 The judges' decision was so important that it changed the way the law was to be interpreted. It was a ....

6 Information about the new drug was given to the press by a laboratory technician. The manager decided to sack him in order to ....

7 The tragic accident .... an otherwise happy event.

8 The major drugs companies need a way to replace the money they earn from patents that are expiring. They need new patents to ....

9 The law about intellectual property is very complex but essential to the success of the company. It finally .... the Managing Director that he should consult a legal expert.

C Definitions

Match these terms with their definitions.

1	permit (line 10)	**a)**	competing
2	excludes (line 19)	**b)**	creativity
3	tissue (line 22)	**c)**	allow
4	rival (line 25)	**d)**	safeguard
5	protect (line 40)	**e)**	aware
6	alert (line 44)	**f)**	skin and flesh
7	investors (line 53)	**g)**	leaves out
8	inventiveness (line 90)	**h)**	people risking money

D Metaphors from water

English uses a lot of metaphors from water to describe the scale of events, like *a flood of complaints* and *a huge wave of research*. Complete these sentences with words from the box.

> drop   flood   trickle   stream   torrents   cascade

1 It was too little, too late – a ......*drop*....... in the ocean.

2 The complaints started off as a .... but soon became a flood.

3 The benefits .... down from the upper management to the whole workforce.

4 There was a steady .... of visitors when the new Centre was opened to the public.

5 The rain fell in such .... you could hardly see well enough to drive.

6 There was a .... of applications for the job when the salary was announced.

E Metaphors from the body

Match the parts of the body with the correct phrase.

1	head	**a)**	of the law
2	long arm	**b)**	for fighting
3	hand	**c)**	of the company
4	heart	**d)**	of Fate
5	no stomach	**e)**	of the matter

Over to you

1 Make a list of the main steps a small research company should take in order to ensure that their discoveries are not stolen or copied.

2 Why do you think the Biotechnology Directive excludes human cloning processes from patentability except for spare parts? What consequences does this have for research companies?

Land ownership

Before you read

Discuss these questions.

1 Who owns the lakes, mountains and rivers in your country? Is there a lot of private land ownership, or does the state control the countryside and 'unclaimed' land? Is it all mapped and registered?

2 Do you think commercial exploitation of the natural resources of the land (for example, minerals) can also respect the traditions of the area where those resources are found?

3 Do you know in which parts of the world gold and uranium are found?

Reading tasks

A Understanding main points

Read the text on the opposite page about a case of land ownership and answer these questions.

1 Who are the main protesters in Australia against ERA?

2 What are the protesters trying to achieve?

3 Who owns the land where the uranium is?

4 For how many years have the Aboriginal people tried to ban the mine?

5 What is the highest court in Australia?

6 What rights do the Aboriginal people claim they have dating from 1976?

7 Do the Aboriginal people consider the contract with the mining companies to be valid?

8 Which company owns ERA?

9 What does the word *stand-off* mean in this context? (line 49)

10 When will mining operations begin?

B Understanding details

Mark these statements T (true) or F (false) according to the information in the text. Find the part of the text that gives the correct information.

1 The Aboriginal and environmental groups succeeded in stopping the mine. *F*

2 A mining lease is an official document that permits free use of land to the owner.

3 ERA is a private company.

4 According to the text, Australia has three main uranium producers.

5 The High Court is the highest court in Australia.

6 The federal court operates at a local, state level.

7 The Aboriginal people have ownership of the land.

8 If an agreement is made when one party is *under duress*, it is not lawful.

Australian Aborigines plan protests over uranium ruling

By Gwen Robinson in Sydney

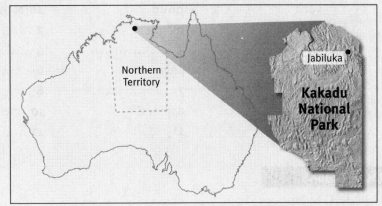

Aboriginal groups and environmentalists are planning protests across Australia after failing to block the development of a uranium mine on traditional Aboriginal land in the Northern Territory. Australia's federal court ruled last week that the territory's government had the right to grant a mining lease at Jabiluka, which lies inside a World Heritage-listed national park, to Energy Resources of Australia (ERA). The company is one of Australia's two uranium producers.

The ruling virtually exhausted the legal options for the Mirrar Aboriginal people in their 20-year-old campaign to block uranium mining on their traditional land at Jabiluka, which contains one of the world's largest undeveloped uranium deposits.

An appeal to the High Court, Australia's supreme judicial authority, is possible but unlikely, considering the weight attached to decisions by the federal court's full bench, analysts said.

The Mirrar group was granted custody of the land under the 1976 Land Rights Act. In recent years it has tried to overturn an earlier agreement between one of its former leaders, now dead, and mining interests. The group says that approval to mine at Jabiluka was given 'under duress'.

After the judgment, environmentalist groups, including Greenpeace and the Wilderness Society, said they would step up their protests, both at Jabiluka and in Australia's main cities, to try to halt development of the mine.

The managing director of North, a diversified mining company and majority owner of ERA, last week described the stand-off as a 'totemic issue'. 'As far as we can see, Jabiluka will stay on track and on timetable and there is no reason that legal challenges would hold it up,' he said.

FINANCIAL TIMES
World business newspaper.

Vocabulary tasks

A Denying permission and prohibition

Use an appropriate word or phrase from the box to complete each sentence.

ban	block	stand-off	stand in the way of	overturned	held up

1 There is a government ....*ban*....... on selling uranium to foreigners.

2 The socialist government .... a previous decision taken by the conservative government relating to uranium mining in Jabiluka.

3 The company has tried to .... attempts to stop it developing the mine.

4 When two parties prevent each other from acting and no one can proceed, it is a ....

5 Greenpeace and the Wilderness Society hope to .... ERA's commercial exploitation of traditional Aboriginal lands.

6 The mining company sees no reason why work should be .... for legal reasons.

B Word families

Complete the chart.

verb	noun	adjective
1 ......*rule*......	ruling	2 ....
regulate	3	4 ....
5	judgment	6 ....
decide	7	8 ....
9	approval	10 ....
permit	11	12 ....

Reading tasks

A Understanding main points

Read the text below about a diamond mine in Canada and answer these questions.

1 Is the mine a commercial success?

2 When did BHP start to develop the mine?

3 Where is the mine located within Canada?

4 What does the mine in Canada extract?

5 Which groups did the company have to negotiate with?

BHP makes a pipe dream come true

Canada's Ekati diamond mine is a triumph of cooperation, writes Scott Morrison.

The Ekati diamond mine sits alongside an important caribou migration route in Canada's desolate Northwest Territories. Grizzly bears and other wild animals are known to pass by occasionally, but the region was rarely visited by man until Broken Hill Proprietary, the Australian group, began developing the site almost two years ago.

The logistical challenges of establishing a mine in the remote region around Lac de Gras, some 300 km north of Yellowknife, were compounded by an inhospitable climate that can send temperatures plummeting to minus 50 degrees Celsius. The mine site was far from ideal and many sceptics believed hopes of extracting diamonds from the Canadian tundra were a pipe dream.

Territorial officials and native leaders acknowledge that BHP was quick to understand that for the project to succeed, the interests of the local population would have to be taken into account. The company spent several years negotiating with the territorial government and four native groups that claimed rights to the territory on which the diamond-bearing pipes were discovered.

Native and territorial leaders were very concerned about protecting the environment and demanded that the company divert waterways, safeguard against environmental damage and maintain the purity of small lakes at the mine site. In possibly the most contentious issue, government leaders demanded that BHP build a sorting and evaluation centre in Yellowknife and sell 10% of the mine's output to buyers within the territory. Native Indians have received training and jobs at the mine as well as financial compensation.

FINANCIAL TIMES
World business newspaper.

B Comparison of the two texts

Use an appropriate word or phrase from the text to complete each sentence.

Similarities

1 Location: Both sites are located in the .... of the country.

2 Land ownership: Both sites are on .... lands.

3 Company ownership: Both companies are ....

4 Government support: Both mines ....

5 Profitability: Uranium and diamond mines are usually very ....

Differences

6 Location: The Ekati mine is in a place where the temperatures are very .... while the Jabiluka mine is in an area where the temperatures are very ....

7 Production: The Australian mine is for .... while the Canadian mine is for ....

8 Cooperation: Native groups have been fully consulted and agree to the development of the .... , but the same is not true at the ....

9 Local interests: In ...., local people will benefit from having jobs in the mine and the produce will be sold locally, but in .... this is not the case.

10 Environmental issues: The government and the company seem very concerned about protecting the environment in ...., but Greenpeace and the Wilderness Society are very worried about the future in ....

Over to you

1 Compare and contrast the two mines from the point of view of: (a) the local people; (b) the mining companies; and (c) the legal position. Quote exactly from the two articles to support your ideas. Use some of the following phrases to introduce quoted evidence:

According to ...

Government leaders said ...

Native groups argued ...

A spokesman for ... said ...

2 Which of the two cases acknowledged the traditional rights of native peoples most satisfactorily? What more should be done, in your opinion?

In confidence

Discuss these questions

1 Can you think of situations where you need to be sure that what you say is in confidence?

2 What business situations can you imagine when confidentiality is a requirement?

A Understanding main points

Read the contract on the opposite page and answer these questions.

1 What is this agreement called?

2 How many parties are involved in the letter of agreement?

3 What do the Company and Princeton have to do to show that they abide by all the conditions?

4 How many definitions are there in the agreement?

5 What will Princeton use the information for?

6 What happens if legal authorities demand to see the confidential information?

7 How long does the agreement last, if no other agreement is made?

8 How can the agreement be changed?

B Understanding details

Answer these questions.

1 Is Target Enterprises the giver or the receiver of the confidential information?

2 What does 'your prior consent' allow Princeton to do, in 1a?

3 Who do the 'representatives' work for – Princeton or Target Enterprises?

4 Which clause mentions the possible destruction of all the written confidential documents?

5 Which clause sets out the fact that no firm contract exists to finalise any deal and that Princeton can stop the discussions at any time?

6 Which clauses explain when information is not considered to be 'confidential'?

7 Is Princeton free to use information that it acquired before signing this agreement?

8 Can it use information in the public domain?

9 Which four institutions are mentioned as possibly requiring the information to be disclosed?

10 How many parties must agree and accept the letter?

Princeton

Target Enterprises, 186 Roydon Street, London SW1
Date:

Dear Sirs
CONFIDENTIALITY UNDERTAKING[1]

1 In consideration of Target Enterprises (hereinafter 'The Company') providing Princeton Limited (hereinafter 'Princeton' 'us' or 'we') with information in relation, *inter alia*, to the business of the Company and the possibility of a transaction relating to the same (collectively, 'Confidential Information'), we hereby undertake to the Company, always subject to paragraph 2 below, as follows:

a) We agree that unless we have obtained your prior written consent, we will not disclose or permit the disclosure to any third party other than our Representatives (as defined in paragraph (b) below), the fact that the Company may be considering a possible transaction with us or with other parties, the fact that certain information has been made available to us regarding the Company, the fact that we and the Company are or may be engaged in discussions with respect to a possible transaction or the status of such discussions; and

b) The Confidential Information will be used solely for the purpose of evaluating, negotiating, advising on or implementing a proposed transaction and will be held in confidence by us and will not be disclosed to any person other than such directors, officers, employees, agents, representatives and advisers of Princeton group of companies (collectively, our 'Representatives')

c) We will upon the written request of the Company deliver to the Company or, at our option, destroy, all written Confidential Information provided to us, including any copies, extracts or other reproductions in whole or in part, of such written material. We will, upon the written request of the Company, use our reasonable endeavours to destroy all documents, memoranda, notes and other writings whatsoever prepared by us or any of our Representatives to the extent containing or reflecting or derived from any Confidential Information or any negotiations or proposals relating to any proposed transaction ('Relevant Material').

d) In the event that we and/or any of our Representatives are required by law, regulation or by any requirement of any regulatory body or other government authority to disclose any Confidential Information, notice of such fact shall be given to The Company by telephone or facsimile.

e) Unless and until a definitive written agreement is executed and delivered by us and the Company, neither we nor The Company shall be under any obligation to complete a transaction contemplated hereby and either we or The Company may, in its sole and absolute discretion, discontinue discussions, negotiations or due diligence related to any potential transaction; and

f) The obligations of each of The Company and Princeton imposed by this letter of undertaking shall cease upon the earlier of the entering into of a binding agreement between The Company and Princeton and the second anniversary of the date hereof; and

g) This letter agreement may not be modified or amended except in the form of a written document executed by the Company and Princeton; and

2 The obligations on us under this letter of undertaking shall not apply:

a) To any information lawfully in the possession of ourselves prior to the supply of the Confidential Information; or

b) To information which enters the public domain after the supply of the Confidential Information for any reason not attributable to any actions of ourselves or our Representatives; or

c) Without prejudice to paragraph 1e above, to information which is required to be disclosed by applicable law or order of court of competent jurisdiction any government department or recognised stock exchange agency or other regulatory body or authority whether or not having the force of law; or

d) To information which is independently developed by us other than in breach of this letter of undertaking.

3 The Company agrees that we are not liable for any costs which the owners of The Company, its directors, employees or their respective advisers may incur in relation to the disclosure of the Confidential Information or any subsequent negotiations.

4 Subject to the express obligations herein, we shall be free to use the Confidential Information free of charge and without limit as to time, territory or manner of disclosure. This letter agreement shall be governed by and construed in accordance with the laws of England.

Yours faithfully,

For and on behalf of Princeton Limited

Agreed and Accepted:

For and on behalf of Target Enterprises
Date:

---

1 This is an abridged extract from a confidentiality agreement and, as such, would not be suitable for use as a legal document.

Legal Brief

An agreement or a contract have no standing in law unless they are signed by all the parties named in the contract, and dated. A letter expressing an undertaking of confidentiality has as much legal force as a more traditional contract.

Vocabulary tasks

A Legal terms

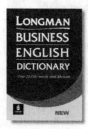

Match these terms with their definitions. Use a good dictionary, such as the *Longman Business English Dictionary*, to help you.

1	disclose (line 10)	a)	right to act in a case
2	reasonable endeavours (line 34)	b)	reveal
3	execute and deliver (line 49)	c)	legal authority
4	absolute discretion (line 53)	d)	possible business deal
5	potential transaction (line 55)	e)	without influence or obligation
6	binding agreement (line 59)	f)	do something which causes expense
7	competent jurisdiction (line 76)	g)	legally responsible
8	force of law (line 80)	h)	make every effort
9	liable (line 83)	i)	draw up and send
10	incur (line 85)	j)	legal obligation

B Contract language

Match these terms and their definitions.

1	in consideration of (line 1)	a)	breaking the agreement
2	hereinafter (line 1)	b)	regarding the fact
3	hereby (line 7)	c)	not affecting existing rights
4	subject to (line 7)	d)	in the absence of
5	at our option (line 29)	e)	before
6	unless and until (line 48)	f)	from now on in this document
7	prior to (line 68)	g)	as a result of this document
8	without prejudice (line 74)	h)	on condition that
9	in breach of (line 82)	i)	understood and interpreted
10	construed (line 92)	j)	according to our choice

C Complete the sentence

Use an appropriate word from the box to complete each sentence.

| hereby   hereinafter   therefore   hereto   herewith |

1 I .....*hereby*..... promise that I will not release any further details about the matter.
   Signed: Mrs Green.

2 The two firms, Brite and Stockdale, ... referred to as the Holder and the Receiver, agree the following.

3 Please find .... three more pages that belong to the brief.

4 This is an urgent matter and .... I ask you to sign and return these papers as soon as possible.

5 Please study the list of prices attached .... and reply immediately to my clerk.

D Use of *shall* in contracts

Legal English is marked by the more formal use of *shall* in legal documents. Complete the sentences with the appropriate form of *shall* or *will*, and re-write each sentence in a simpler, more everyday style.

1 'Confidential information' ......*shall*...... mean all information disclosed.

   Confidential information means all information made available to the reader.

2 What time .... you be back this evening?

3 Nothing in this document .... be construed as granting any rights to the Company.

4 The Company .... promptly destroy all materials if so requested.

5 If you carry the boxes, I .... carry the bags.

6 Princeton .... bear no responsibility for the accuracy of the information.

7 What do you think he .... say when he hears the news?

8 The Company .... not make any reference to the materials without the permission of the firm.

Over to you

1 Have you ever seen a contract, such as a marriage contract or a contract of employment ? Who signs them and what happens if the contracts are broken? Where can you find examples of contracts to study? Try looking on the Internet, or at your local Citizens Advice office, or in your library. Research and make a short report on your findings.

2 Imagine that you and a partner have invented a product or service to sell. Write a letter to your lawyer, asking for some advice on drawing up a simple, clear and easy to understand contract between you and your partner, since you have only have a verbal agreement.

Licences

Discuss these questions.

1 How do international companies organise the production of their goods outside their own markets? What alternatives do they have?

2 Have you ever bought a drink with a famous brand name, that you know has been produced locally? How many brand items can you think of that are made under licence in your country?

3 Apart from famous brands of clothing or drinks, what other kinds of business may be performed under licence?

A Understanding main points

Read the extract on the opposite page from a licence agreement between two publishers and answer these questions.

1 What kind of publication does this licence agreement permit the Publishers to produce?

2 When does the agreement come into effect?

3 Can the Publishers make any changes to the original version?

4 What assurances do the Proprietors give that there will be no legal problems with copyright?

5 If the licence is to be extended to other parties, what must be done?

6 Can the licence be renewed by only one party?

7 What action must be taken if there is a dispute about the agreement?

8 In the worst case, what will happen if the parties cannot agree?

B Understanding details

Answer these questions.

1 Is there any reference to payment in the agreement? If so, which clause is it in?

2 What do *they* and *it* refer to in lines 18–19?

3 What is meant by *this warranty* in line 31?

4 What are *the rights and liabilities* of the parties in line 40?

5 What does *the same* refer to in line 40?

6 What is an *umpire*, as referred to in line 42?

7 Is there any difference in the text in clause 8 between *difference* and *dispute*?

8 What two phrases are used to show that the 1996 Act may be changed in the future?

MEMORANDUM OF AGREEMENT

made this ..... day of .... 20......

Between .... of .... (hereinafter termed the

Publishers) of one part and .... of ....

5 (hereinafter termed the Proprietors) of the other part

WHEREAS the Proprietors are the proprietors of a work

entitled: .... (hereinafter termed the Work),

NOW IT IS HEREBY MUTUALLY AGREED AS FOLLOWS:

1. Subject to the terms detailed in this Agreement, the Proprietors hereby grant to
10 the Publishers the exclusive licence to produce and publish a single printing of
10,000 copies only of the Work in paperback form in the English language under the
Publishers' own imprint[1] (hereinafter termed the Licensed Edition) for sale
throughout .... only. This restricted circulation is to be clearly indicated on
the outside of the cover and on the reverse of the title page[2] of the Licensed Edition
15 by the following words: "Licensed for sale in .... only; not for export."

2. This agreement shall not come into effect until the Proprietors have received the
(advance) payment detailed in Clause 9 hereof.

3. The Publishers shall produce the Licensed Edition at their own expense. They
shall cause it to be reproduced faithfully and accurately and shall not abridge,
20 expand or otherwise alter the Work, including illustrations where applicable,
without the prior written consent of the Proprietors.

4. Should the Publishers fail to issue the Licensed Edition within 12 months from
the date of this Agreement all rights granted under this Agreement shall revert to
the Proprietors without prejudice to any monies paid or due to the Proprietors.

25 **5.** The Proprietors hereby warrant to the Publishers that they have the right and
power to make this Agreement and that according to English law the Work will in
no way whatever give rise to a violation of any existing copyright, or a breach of
any existing agreement and that nothing in the Work is liable to give rise to a civil
prosecution or to a civil action for damages or any other remedy and the Proprietors
30 will indemnify the Publishers against any loss, injury or expense arising out of any
breach of this warranty.

6. The Licence hereby granted to the Publishers shall not be transferred in whole or
in part or extended to include any other party nor shall the Licensed Edition appear
under any imprint other than that of the Publishers, except with the prior written
35 consent of the Proprietors.

7. The Licence herein granted shall continue for a period of five years from the date
of first publication by the Publishers of the Licensed Edition and thereafter may be
subject to renewal by mutual agreement between the parties hereto.

8. If any difference shall arise between the Proprietors and the Publishers touching
40 the meaning of this Agreement or the rights and liabilities of the parties hereto, the
same shall be referred to the arbitration of two persons (one to be named by each
party) or their umpire, in accordance with the provisions of the Arbitration Act 1996
or any subsisting statutory modification or re-enactment thereof, provided that any
dispute between the parties hereto not resolved by arbitration or agreement shall be
submitted to the jurisdiction of the English courts.

1 a publisher's trademark

2 usually the first page in the book

From *Publishing Agreements*, Butterworth

Legal brief

Copyright is a legal term used to show the rights of ownership of creative ideas, originally for published literary works but later extended to include such things as music and motion pictures. New legislation is now needed to deal with the increasing use of the Internet and issues arising from abuses of intellectual property rights. In the EU, copyright protection lasts for 70 years after the death of the copyright holder. There are criminal penalties for infringement of copyright.

Vocabulary tasks

A Definitions

Match these legal terms from the licence agreement with their definitions.

1	memorandum	a)	give
2	hereinafter termed	b)	change
3	subject to	c)	written record
4	grant	d)	limited to
5	exclusive	e)	so-called in the agreement after this definition
6	come into effect	f)	depending on
7	abridge, expand, alter	g)	return to
8	prior written consent	h)	concerning the interpretation
9	revert to	i)	breaking the law of authors' rights
10	without prejudice to any monies paid	j)	legal authority
11	hereby warrant	k)	guarantee
12	right and power	l)	will be sent
13	violation of copyright	m)	regardless of any payments made
14	touching the meaning	n)	will be applied
15	shall be submitted	o)	previous written permission

34

B Complete the sentence

Use an appropriate word or phrase from Exercise A to complete each sentence.

1 The agreement specified that the Proprietors were legally entitled to the ownership of all rights in the book. They had the ...*right and power*... to make the agreement.

2 Bookbinders Inc (.................. the Publishers) and Jones and Company (.................. the Proprietors) hereby mutually agree the following.

3 This agreement is for five years and shall .... after the agreed payment has been made.

4 The rights granted in this agreement are .... to the licence holder.

5 No changes shall be made to this agreement without the .... of the Proprietors.

6 If any difference shall arise between the Proprietors and the Publishers .... of this Agreement, the same shall be referred to arbitration.

7 .... the satisfactory performance of the licence holder, this agreement may be renewed.

8 Should the licence holder fail to fulfil all the requirements of the agreement, all rights shall .... the Proprietors.

C Word search

Replace the underlined items with words and phrases from the text that have a similar meaning.

1 This agreement is issued by the <u>owners</u> of the rights.   *Proprietors*

2 The terms are <u>described</u> in this agreement.

3 Publishing this book will <u>certainly not</u> cause any legal difficulties for either party.

4 The Proprietors will <u>protect</u> the licence holder against any expense.

5 The agreement may not be <u>altered to involve</u> any other person.

Over to you

1 Prepare a business letter to a law expert asking him or her to explain the licence agreement in simple terms. Make specific reference to the points you do not understand, such as the arrangements for arbitration.

2 Think about the licensed goods available in your country. Examine any examples you can find and list the physical signs you can identify (on labels, or on packaging, inside or out) that a licence has been used, or perhaps not used, legally. Then write a brief report.

Fraud

Discuss these questions.

1 How does an investor find out about new and exciting opportunities? How reliable do you think investment advice available in newspapers is?

2 'Money for nothing' and 'get rich quick' schemes are often really confidence tricks. Has any one ever suggested that you invest in a particular scheme?

Reading tasks

A Understanding main points

Read the text on the opposite page about a gold mine fraud and answer these questions.

1 How much gold did Bre-X say they had found in Indonesia back in February 1996?

2 What was the market capitalisation of Bre-X before the scandal?

3 Where are the courtroom dramas being played out?

4 How many investors are being represented by lawyers against Bre-X?

5 Who do the prosecuting lawyers think should be held accountable for the fiasco?

6 Why is the case so critical to brokerages in the US?

7 Is this case setting a precedent if the investors win?

8 Which firms are accused of being involved in the fraud?

9 What is the Canadian gold producer Barrick accused of doing?

10 Why don't the cheated investors sue Bre-X?

B Information search

Look quickly at the graph and dates on the opposite page and answer these questions.

1 What was the basis for the belief that there was a huge gold deposit in Busang?

2 What did the exploration predict about Bre-X?

3 What happened on 19 March to Mr Guzman?

4 What happened to Bre-X shares on 26 March?

5 Why did the computer crash on 1 April?

6 Which organisation revealed they were investigating Bre-X on 3 April?

7 What evidence was there that there was no gold after all?

Bre-X Minerals drama continues in the courts

It is now some time since the Busang gold deposit was revealed as a hoax. **Scott Morrison** examines the effects on the mining industry and the legal battle still being fought by investors.

More than three years have passed since Bre-X Minerals' purported 71m ounce gold deposit in Indonesia was unmasked as nothing more than an elaborate hoax.

When the dust settled, the Canadian company's C$6bn (US$4.2bn) market capitalisation had been wiped out and Bre-X's worthless shares were de-listed.

The drama, which unfolded first in the jungles of Borneo and later on in stock markets in North America, is now being played out in courtrooms in Toronto and in a remote corner of Texas, where lawyers have launched lawsuits seeking billions of dollars in damages.

While there is little doubt that Bre-X perpetrated a massive scam, lawyers representing some 2,000 investors say the company and its directors are not the only ones to be held accountable. The lawsuits also allege that several brokerage firms issued false and misleading reports about the Busang deposit and profited from their association with the company. The plaintiffs' arguments, if they are successful, could set a chilling precedent for the entire brokerage industry.

In Canada, the efforts of investors to seek redress took a significant step forward in March when a judge ruled that plaintiffs could proceed with a lawsuit against Bre-X, its officials, engineering firms and brokerage houses. The defendants have said they will appeal the ruling.

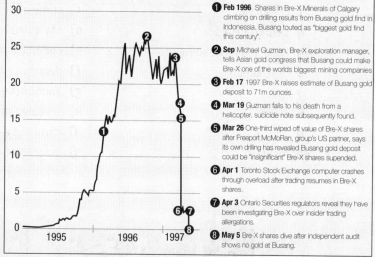

1. **Feb 1996** Shares in Bre-X Minerals of Calgary climbing on drilling results from Busang gold find in Indonesia. Busang touted as "biggest gold find this century".

2. **Sep** Michael Guzman, Bre-X exploration manager, tells Asian gold congress that Busang could make Bre-X one of the worlds biggest mining companies

3. **Feb 17** 1997 Bre-X raises estimate of Busang gold deposit to 71m ounces.

4. **Mar 19** Guzman falls to his death from a helicopter. suicide note subsequently found.

5. **Mar 26** One-third wiped off value of Bre-X shares after Freeport McMoRan, group's US partner, says its own drilling has revealed Busang gold deposit could be "insignificant" Bre-X shares supended.

6. **Apr 1** Toronto Stock Exchange computer crashes through overload after trading resumes in Bre-X shares.

7. **Apr 3** Ontario Securities regulators reveal they have been investigating Bre-X over insider trading allergations.

8. **May 5** Bre-X shares dive after independent audit shows no gold at Busang.

The legal actions pit small investors against nine of the top brokerage houses in North America. The case alleges that brokerages were negligent in issuing misleading statements proclaiming the company's Busang gold deposits as the largest in the world, and that they also participated in 'a fraud on the market', a procedural doctrine under US law.

However, a renowned securities law expert in the US has said that extending responsibility for fraud to 'aiders and abettors' – in this case the brokerages that recommended Bre-X stock – would prove difficult. The US lawsuit also alleges that Barrick, the Canadian gold producer that tried to negotiate a partnership with Bre-X, disseminated false statements or concealed materially adverse facts. Barrick claim it was prevented from disclosing the results of its due diligence because it signed a confidentiality agreement.

It is far from clear that plaintiff attorneys will succeed in their attempts to hold brokerages liable for the Bre-X fiasco. If they succeed, it would be the first time legislation against false advertising was applied to securities. Many observers say they have little choice other than to sue deep-pocketed brokerages that promoted the stock, because Bre-X itself is bankrupt and company insiders who profited from the fraud could not cover billions of dollars in claims.

FINANCIAL TIMES
World business newspaper.

Vocabulary tasks

A Words relating to fraud

Match these terms with their definitions.

1	purported	a)	people in a company with access to privileged information
2	unmasked	b)	said to be true, but really false
3	elaborate	c)	crime of deception and deceit
4	perpetrate a scam	d)	say something is true
5	false and misleading reports	e)	complicated
6	proclaiming	f)	disaster, a failure
7	fraud	g)	announcing publicly
8	claim	h)	revealed as false
9	fiasco	i)	carry out a dishonest scheme to make money
10	insiders	j)	inaccurate statements

"Ah, Mr Jenkins, you're probably wondering about those mining shares I told you to buy last month ..."

B Legal language

Match these terms with their definitions.

1 damages a) people who bring a case to court
2 accountable b) financial compensation
3 precedent c) people accused of a crime in a court case
4 seek redress d) case that sets rules
5 plaintiffs e) sue to regain losses
6 defendants f) promise to keep something secret
7 negligent g) having to explain and justify
8 due diligence h) legally responsible
9 confidentiality agreement i) thorough check
10 liable j) not do a job professionally

C Word search

Find a word or phrase in the text that has a similar meaning.

1 take a bankrupt company's shares off the stock exchange (para 2)
   de-list

2 firms that buy and sell shares on behalf of clients (para 4)
   b..................

3 people who have only modest amounts of money to spend on shares (para 6)
   s.................. i..................

4 when a company deliberately misleads the public (para 6)
   p.................. in a f.................. on the m..................

5 people who help each other to commit a crime (para 7)
   a.................. and a..................

6 government bonds, holdings, stocks and shares (para 8)
   s..................

Over to you

1 Do you think the small investors will win their case in the gold scam? On what grounds? Are there other factors to stop small groups winning against bigger ones?

2 The chart shows a dramatic rise and fall in the share price of Bre-X Minerals between June 1995 and May 1997. Read the eight-point diary by the chart and then describe what happened. Use the past tense to tell the story.

Telephone crime

Before you read

Discuss these questions.

1 How many telephone calls do you make every day? Do you have a telephone calling card?

2 How often do you call someone living outside your country? Are these personal or business calls? How do you pay for such calls?

Reading tasks

A Understanding main points

Read the text on the opposite page about telephone fraud and answer these questions.

1 Who pays the bills when there is telephone crime?

2 What is BT's calling card division?

3 How much does telephone crime cost operators a year?

4 How many fraudulent calls are made each year according to trade organisations?

5 Is telephone crime mainly committed by professional criminals or bored youngsters?

6 What is the simplest example of telephone crime mentioned in the text?

7 How does BT plan to protect itself from fraud?

8 How has new technology helped BT solve crimes?

B Understanding details

What do the following figures refer to in the text?

1 $334m   2 55,000   3 400,000   4 £2m   5 120m

C Complete the sentence

Use an appropriate word from the text to complete the six stages of a telephone crime.

1 A criminal has to open an ...*account*...... .

2 Next, he has to give a .... name.

3 The crime consists of making contact with people who need to .... a lot of expensive phone calls but have little money.

4 These people agree to .... the criminal in cash for the calls they make – not the real costs of course, much less.

5 The criminal then sells hundreds of long- .... phone calls – to Australia, for example.

6 However, when the bill is .... at the end of the month, the criminal disappears.

FINANCIAL TIMES   MONDAY JULY 6 ★★   BRITAIN

BT launches fresh attack on phone crime

By Alan Cane

British Telecommunications (BT) is mounting a new offensive against the barons of organised telephone crime who are costing it hundreds of millions of pounds annually. Its chief weapon is a new technology that can cut the time to detect and prove fraud from – in some cases – years to minutes. Developed with BT's former partner, MCI of the US, the system has already been tested by BT's calling card division, where it has doubled the number of frauds spotted and halved the financial losses. Now it is being deployed across BT's business services.

The level of UK phone crime is hard to assess, but it is costing operators a minimum of £200m ($334m) a year. Trade organisations put the figure at 55,000 crimes reported, with a similar number of unreported fraudulent calls. And forget youngsters and amateurs: telephone fraud is big-time crime. Some of the UK's best-known villains are defrauding the operators to fund activities ranging from drugs to terrorism, according to Dennis Gotts, head of BT's investigations unit. 'This is more than stealing 10p from a call box,' he says. 'Notorious individuals in the criminal fraternity are involved. They know BT's network and they know what they are doing.'

Telephone crime can be absurdly easy. Opening an account in a false name and selling calls to international destinations before disappearing when the bill is due is one of the simplest. In one case earlier this year, a gang of Tamil sympathisers siphoned off or diverted some £2m from 400,000 fraudulent calls to Sri Lanka before they were arrested, convicted and imprisoned.

It took BT's investigators two years to collect the evidence to put the gang on trial. The new system, called 'Sheriff', will be able to do the job in minutes. Detection involves analysis of hundreds of millions of call records looking for unusual patterns: an unexpectedly large number of calls to a particular number or destination, for example, or calls made at unusual hours or from unusual locations.

BT's fraud strategy manager said the company's services were already protected, but by individual systems. The need was for a single system so fraud alert data could be shared across product lines.

Sheriff uses artificial intelligence for analysis and an advanced 'object-orientated' database from Versant, a US company, to provide the speed and reliability needed to sort through a minimum of 120m calls a day on BT's network. The system 'learns' from its experiences, so improving its ability to detect future frauds.

BT is considering offering a tailored fraud-detection service to its large corporate customers.

FINANCIAL TIMES
World business newspaper.

Vocabulary tasks

A References

Who or what do the underlined words refer to?
1 who are costing (line 4)   *the barons of organised telephone crime*
2 Its chief weapon (line 6)
3 where it has doubled the number of frauds (line 13)
4 This is more than stealing 10p from a call box (line 32)
5 they know what they are doing (line 37)
6 before they were arrested (line 49)
7 its ability to detect fraud (line 78)
8 to its large corporate customers (line 81)

B Word search

Replace the underlined items with words and phrases from the text that have a similar meaning.

1 BT is preparing a new <u>attack</u> against telephone fraud. (para 1)

o*ffensive*........

2 The system has <u>increased the number of detected crimes.</u> (para 1)

d................... the n................... of f................... s...................

3 Telephone fraud is <u>very serious</u>. (para 2)

b...................-t................... c...................

4 One form of the crime is selling calls to others and <u>then failing to meet the bill.</u> (para 3)

d................... w................... the b................... is d...................

5 BT experts took two years to find enough evidence to <u>take the criminals to court.</u> (para 4)

p................... the g................... on t...................

6 The system uses an <u>advanced computer programme that identifies patterns of calls.</u> (para 6)

a................... o...................-o................... d...................

7 The company may offer a fraud-detection service to its business customers that is <u>specially designed for each customer</u>. (para 7)

t...................

C Complete the sentence

Use an appropriate word or phrase from the box to complete each sentence.

> detect   prove   barons of organised crime   fraud   false name
> evidence   arrested   convicted   imprisoned

1 It is one thing to .....*detect*....... fraud; it is quite another to .... it.

2 Telephone .... is said to be in the hands of ....

3 The police cannot prosecute a criminal without ....

4 One gang managed to steal millions before they were ...., ... and
....

5 Opening an account in a .... seems to be very simple.

D Definitions

Match these terms with their definitions.

1 siphon off and divert   **a)** hold someone at a police station

2 arrest   **b)** implement a serious campaign against an enemy

3 convict   **c)** move part of something without the owner knowing about it

4 imprison   **d)** put someone in prison

5 mount an offensive   **e)** find someone guilty of a crime

E Word fields

Write these words in the appropriate columns.

murder arson robbery assault fraud forgery perjury burglary money laundering rape kidnapping bribery blackmail

crimes against people   **other crimes**

.............*murder*..............   ....*arson*............

....

....

....

....

....

....

Over to you

1 You discover that a colleague at work has been involved in telephone crime – she has opened an account in a false name and is selling calls to other office workers. Write a letter to your boss explaining what has been going on, and how you discovered it.

2 'Organised crime' – groups of notorious criminals – are involved in telephone crime, according to the text. What can international police forces do to prevent their activities? Think about such things as cross-border cooperation, sharing of information, developing specialised technology (like the call monitoring device Sheriff), and list the actions that could help stop international telephone crime.

Money laundering

Before you read

Discuss these questions.

1 Is it easy or difficult in your country to conceal financial transactions from the 'tax man'? Is there a strong 'black' economy?

2 Are you familiar with the concept of 'laundering' money – turning 'dirty' money into 'clean' funds? Where does the 'dirty' money come from? Is it always criminal activity?

3 Can bank transfers conceal stolen or embezzled funds?

Reading tasks

A Understanding main points

Read the text on the opposite page about how organised crime uses the international banking system to hide its money and answer these questions.

1 Where did the police arrest the Mexican money launderers?

2 How many people were arrested in total?

3 What was Operation Casablanca designed to do?

4 How much drug money is thought to be laundered world-wide every year?

5 According to the UN Drugs report, how much is the illegal drugs business worth every year?

6 How much can be recovered through anti-laundering measures?

7 How is it that more and more money can be laundered? What systems are used?

8 Do criminals have to abide by the same rules as legitimate bank customers?

9 How do criminals hide their financial transactions from officials?

10 What are the legitimate reasons for bank secrecy?

B Understanding details

Answer these questions.

1 What is meant by *megabyte money*?

2 What are *aggregate funds* normally used for?

3 Why do UN officials want to make banking riskier?

4 Who are the *shareholders and beneficiaries*?

5 What is meant by a *walking* account?

6 Why has the number of banks increased so much?

7 What must a bank have in order to be established, in certain places?

8 What is the favourite way of transporting illegal funds?

9 Why are casinos so popular for money laundering?

10 What can the casino offer to do with the 'winnings'?

World banking system is a 'money launderers' dream'

Report says the ease and speed of 'megabyte money' make it simple to conceal crooked cash, writes **Ian Hamilton Fazey**

It was the biggest money laundering investigation in US history. Evidence had been gathered secretly over many months by undercover officers risking their lives. The suspects were lured to Las Vegas for a conference on money laundering. Then the police struck, arresting 22 banking officials from Mexico's largest financial institution, plus 14 alleged members of Mexican and Colombian drug cartels and another 70 linked to them. Seizure warrants were issued to recover $122m (£73m) from bank accounts in the US and Italy, to add to $35m seized so far. The operation so damaged confidence in Mexican banks that their shares fell collectively by 4% in panic selling.

But as Operation Casablanca struck its blow in the Americas, officials of the United Nations Drug Control Programme in Vienna were editing the final version of a report – to be released soon – that puts the US triumph into a gloomy perspective.

It says that at least $200bn of drug money is laundered every year, but with the illegal international drug trade valued at $500bn, this is probably a conservative estimate. In a good year, up to $500m will be recovered through anti-money laundering measures – an annual success rate of about a quarter of 1% of laundered funds. Operation Casablanca, with $157m, will probably make the year a good one, but hardly vintage.

The report has been prepared by a group of experts for a special session of the UN General Assembly on drugs in New York. With the growth of the international drug trade, more ill-gotten money is being laundered than ever, partly on the back of electronic banking and the increasing globalisation and speed of operation of the international financial system.

Cashless transactions, electronic trading and computerised clearing mean that what the report calls 'megabyte money' can be moved anywhere with speed and ease. With 700,000 wire transfers worth $2,000bn every day, the report says it is 'a reasonable guess that 0.05% to 0.1% contain laundered funds to a value of $300m'. And even though half the total volume of transactions are bank-to-bank transfers of 'aggregate funds' for settlement or loans, the report says the 'complicity of corrupted bank employees' ensures these also contain laundered money. 'This system is a money launderer's dream.'

The one thing law enforcement officers have on their side is that criminals have to play by the rules of the system in order to use it. While it is impossible to spot transactions in progress once money is in the system, criminals have to risk exposure in putting it there. UN officials want the process made riskier.

At present, criminals reduce their risk by operating through offshore financial havens with lax financial regulation and poor banking supervision. They also hide behind banking secrecy, and disguise the ownership of assets by setting up shell companies and offshore trusts in jurisdictions where no questions are asked about shareholders and beneficiaries. Many accounts and trusts are known as 'walking' ones, where there is a standing instruction to move the accounts to another jurisdiction at the first sign of inquiry by the authorities.

UN officials accept that commercial confidentiality, legal tax avoidance and the easing of capital transfers at low or nil tax rates are legitimate reasons for bank secrecy and disguising corporate ownership, but they say the system is too lax in some places, allowing infiltration for illicit or nefarious purposes. 'One of the most striking things about offshore financial centres is the enormous increase that has taken place in the number of banks,' says the report. Banks can be set up with relative speed and ease and a minimum of due diligence investigation, so long as they meet a basic level of funds, which can vary between one jurisdiction and another.

Exporting bulk cash, usually in $100 bills and sometimes carried under diplomatic cover, is the favoured method of getting deposits to banks where no questions will be asked. Casinos in offshore centres are a favourite for converting funds: cash is exchanged for gambling chips, the launderer plays for a while at the tables then exchanges the chips back again. Instead of a cheque, some casinos offer immediate electronic transfer of 'winnings' to an offshore bank account.

FINANCIAL TIMES
World business newspaper.

Vocabulary tasks

A Word search

Find a word in the text to complete these phrases.

1 m *oney* .... laundering (para 1)

2 seizure w.................. (para 1)

3 f................... version (para 2)

4 c.................. estimate (para 3)

5 i...................-g................... money (para 4)

6 e.................. trading (para 5)

7 risk e...................(para 6)

8 f.................. havens (para 7)

9 c.................. confidentiality (para 8)

10 c.................. transfers (para 8)

11 o.................. financial centres (para 8)

12 gambling c................... (para 9)

B Definitions

Match the phrases from Exercise A with their definitions.

1 disguising criminal money by concealing its origins . *money laundering* .

2 keeping business secrets ....

3 in danger of discovery ....

4 papers authorising the authorities to take money or property ....

5 moving large amounts of money from one place to another ....

6 buying and selling through computers ....

7 places where laws and tax are especially lenient ....

8 financial services located in small countries or on islands ....

9 minimum guess ....

10 publishable form ....

11 money obtained illegally ....

12 tokens for playing in casinos ....

C Scrambled words

Use the definitions in the first column to unscramble the words from the text.

1	washing and ironing	unindrelag	*laundering*
2	attract or tempt	rule	....
3	supposed to be true, but not proved	dgladlee	....
4	get back	vecorer	....
5	harm	maadge	....
6	depressing	moogly	....
7	identify	tops	....
8	hide something by making it look different	guisised	....
9	illegal	clitili	....
10	wagering	laminbgg	....

Over to you

1 Write a short description of how money can be laundered. What kinds of activities lend themselves to the easy disposal of cash into legitimate business?

2 Read in the press any new developments on this theme, and comment on them to your class or write up a summary.

Mexican protesters pretend to wash and iron money as part of their campaign against money laundering

Cyberspace fraud

Discuss these questions.

1 Have you ever bought anything through the Internet? If so, what did you buy?

2 How did you pay for the goods you bought? Did you receive them safely?

3 What guarantee did you have that you would get what you paid for?

A Understanding main points

Read the text on the opposite page about Internet fraud and answer these questions.

1 What are the main types of investment fraud reported in the text?

2 How does the text define *cyberspace*?

3 Which four uses of the Internet does the text mention?

4 Anonymity – not being identified, or traced by your real name – is important for criminals. How does the Internet help them ?

5 Which organisations could you inform if you were a victim of a scam on the Internet?

6 Which crime has increased most in the last year or so, according to the text?

7 Do most victims of fraud use traditional payment methods?

8 What does the acronym IFW stand for?

9 An escrow service is a safe way of paying for Internet transactions. How does this work?

B Understanding details

Answer these questions.

1 How do households get exposed to fraudulent schemes in cyberspace?

2 How can the price of stocks and shares be easily manipulated over the Internet?

3 What are the five most common types of Internet fraud, according to Internet Fraud Watch?

4 Mail and telemarketing fraud pre-dated Internet fraud. True or false?

5 Are cyberspace frauds really any different from frauds committed through more traditional communication channels?

ONLINE AUCTIONS NAMED THE NUMBER ONE INTERNET FRAUD COMPLAINT FOR 1998

Cyberspace fraud and abuse

Unwary investors are in danger today of being taken for a ride on the information superhighway.

State securities regulators around the US are concerned about the explosion in illicit investment schemes now flourishing on commercial bulletin board services and the informal web of computer networks that make up the Internet. Households that already have access to online services are being exposed to hundreds of fraudulent and abusive investment schemes including stock manipulations, pyramid scams and Ponzi schemes[1].

Cyberspace, as the online world is known, has the potential to educate investors and help them become better consumers. Any computer and modem is a few keystrokes away from research data and financial news. However, State securities regulators emphasise that the problem of illicit and abusive online investment schemes has the potential to spread like wildfire through the Internet, using increasingly popular commercial bulletin board services, live discussion groups (chats), e-mail, and information web pages, all of which can maintain the anonymity of cyberspace. This is exploited to the hilt by those who promote fraudulent investment schemes.

New frauds are emerging, too. According to Internet Fraud Watch, complaints about fraud on the Internet have risen 600% since 1997, and online auction complaints were the number one fraud complaint only one year later, a dramatic rise. The majority of payments in these fraud cases were made offline, by cheque or money order sent to the company. 'Requesting cash is a clear sign of fraud. Pay the safest way. If possible, pay by credit card because you can dispute the charges if there is a problem,' says the Director of Internet Fraud Watch. IFW recommends that buyers use escrow services: they take payment from the buyers and only pass money along to the sellers after verification that the goods or services were satisfactory. Some auction companies have programmes to insure transactions.

The top 10 scams were, according to the National Consumer League:

1 Web auctions: items bid for but never delivered by the sellers, the value of items inflated, shills[2] suspected of driving up bids;
2 General merchandise: sales of everything from T-shirts to toys, calendars and collectibles, goods never delivered or not as advertised;
3 Internet services: charges for services that were supposedly free, payment made online and Internet services that were never provided or were falsely represented;
4 Hardware or software computer equipment: sales of computer products that were never delivered or were misrepresented;
5 Business opportunities like multi-level marketing or pyramid schemes, in which any profits were made from recruiting others, not from sales of goods and services to end-users;
6 Business opportunities or franchises: empty promises of big profits with little or no work by investing in pre-packaged businesses or franchise opportunities;
7 Work-at-home plans: materials and equipment sold with the false promise of payment for 'piece work' performed at home;
8 Advance fee loans: promises of loans contingent on the consumer paying a large fee in advance. Once the fee is paid, the loans are never disbursed;
9 Credit 'repair': fraudulent promises to remove accurate but negative information from consumer credit reports;
10 Credit card issuing: false promises of credit cards to people with bad credit histories on payment of up-front fees.

1 buyers are persuaded to invest money in dishonest 'businesses' in return for promises of quick profits
2 someone who cooperates in an auction scam by pretending to want to buy goods and so raising the bids

From *www.fraud.org*, The National Consumer League

Legal brief

The National Fraud Information Centre was set up in 1992 to fight telemarketing fraud. In 1996 the National Consumers League in the US decided to expand its efforts to cover fraud in cyberspace. By contacting the website at www.fraud.org, consumers from all over the world can get tips on how to avoid 'scams' (fraudulent tricks) and can report fraud. The site receives 70,000 visits and 1,300 e-mails weekly.

C Definitions

Match the definitions with the scams listed (1–10) in the text.

a) charging for Internet services that are supposed to be free or which fail to appear *3*

b) promising loans of large sums of money after a small fee has been received

c) tempting people to invest in franchise businesses by promising quick profits

d) getting people involved in schemes that work by recruiting a network of other salespeople but not selling any goods

e) selling materials for making-up at home but never selling the things which clients have made

f) falsely guaranteeing that bad credit ratings can be removed from the records

g) taking money for falsely promising credit cards to people with bad-risk ratings

h) receiving money for all kinds of goods that are never delivered

i) selling computer equipment that fails to arrive or is not what was ordered

j) auctioning goods online then not sending the goods, or sending faulty or overpriced articles

Vocabulary tasks

A Understanding expressions

Choose the best explanation for each of these words or phrases from the text.

1 illicit
  a) unhealthy
  b) legal
  c) against the law

2 stock manipulations
  a) moving cattle
  b) selling securities
  c) illegally influencing share prices

3 spread like wildfire
  a) destroy by fire
  b) spread very rapidly
  c) lose your temper

4 to the hilt
  a) to maximum advantage
  b) part time
  c) electronically

5 piece work
  a) working for the community
  b) working in a factory
  c) being paid for each item produced

6 contingent on
  a) in front of
  b) dependent on
  c) next to

7 disbursed
  a) paid money out
  b) collected money
  c) advertised

8 up-front fees
  a) fees that increase as time passes
  b) money paid after receiving goods
  c) money paid before receiving goods

B Complete the sentence

Use an appropriate word from the box to complete each sentence.

> regulations misrepresentation false faulty rulings
> redress liable fines counterfeiting fraudulent

1 The EC hopes to agree on the ..*regulations*.. that will govern the Internet in Europe.

2 The courts made two important .... on the Internet and free speech in the US.

3 There must be ways to seek .... for losses suffered because of electronic fraud.

4 There will be attempts to prevent .... trading.

5 When an issuer is found to be in the wrong, they will be .... for some form of compensation to the victim.

6 In the US, very heavy .... have been levied on certain abusers of the Internet.

7 The Commission is also keen to prevent crimes of forgery like ....

8 Many victims receive goods which are different from what they expect – the sellers are guilty of ....

9 Other cases are when the goods received are .... and do not work.

10 Some credit cards can be issued under a .... name.

C Terms of payment

Use an appropriate phrase from the box to complete each sentence.

> in advance cheque money order credit card escrow fund
> offline payments money up-front advance loan fees

1 A sure sign of a fraud is when you are asked to pay for the goods or services ..*in advance*.., that is before you receive them.

2 Can I pay by .... or .... ?

3 E-commerce chiefly operates with ....

4 .... is the same as paying in advance, isn't it?

5 What is the difference between a .... and a cheque?

6 The safest way to pay for expensive items is to open an ....

7 One scam works by asking for .... but in the end, no loan is given.

Over to you

1 Write a report for your colleagues at work or school warning them of the dangers of electronic commerce. Describe the different crimes you have read about.

2 'My word is my bond' used to be a guarantee of trust and honest trading between people, so that no written contract was needed. Is this still true today? Who would you trust on the Internet? How can you check on a business or individual? Make notes to discuss.

13 | The Magic Kingdom

Before you read

1 Discuss these questions.

a) Can you name any of the best-selling animated films by Walt Disney Studios?

b) What do you know about the contractual and legal aspects of film-making? Who do you suppose makes most money from successful films: the owners of the studio? the actors? the distributors?

c) Do you know what a *bonus clause* in a contract is?

2 Match these terms with their definitions.

1 clause		**a)**	harmless, not dangerous
2 written into		**b)**	part of a contract, stating a condition
3 plaintiff		**c)**	extension or continuation of a previous agreement
4 settlement		**d)**	included, as part of a contract
5 up to date		**e)**	reaching an agreement by discussion and compromise
6 contract renewal		**f)**	agreement that ends a dispute
7 court hearings		**g)**	claimant in a civil trial
8 innocuous		**h)**	informed of the most recent developments
9 negotiating		**i)**	legal action or trial
10 case		**j)**	exploratory legal proceedings to establish if there are grounds for a full trial

Reading tasks

A Understanding main points

Mark these statements T (true) or F (false) according to the information in the text on the opposite page. Find the part of the text that gives the correct information.

1 The legal issue related to a new contract between the Disney company and Jeffrey Katzenberg. **F**

2 His first contract was written in 1984 and said he would receive part of future profits whether he stayed as an employee or not.

3 Katzenberg was studio head for 10 years.

4 Katzenberg said he was owed $580m.

5 Lawyers disagreed that Katzenberg was entitled to profits from films made while he was studio chief.

6 For several years, Disney Corporation did not make profits.

7 Under Katzenberg's leadership, Disney Corporation made $312bn.

8 The most profitable film Katzenberg made was *The Lion King* in 1994.

Inside the Magic Kingdom

By Christopher Parkes

The note to Michael D. Eisner, chairman of Walt Disney Corporation, looked innocuous enough. 'To MDE – just to keep you up to date – probably worth a quick read,' said the lines slanting across a copy of a letter from Frank Wells, group president. The Wells letter – dated 17 October 1988 – was addressed to a lawyer negotiating a contract renewal for Jeffrey Katzenberg, the studio chief behind *The Lion King* and other successes that in the following years established Disney as Hollywood's leading film-maker.

In the middle of seven pages of contractual jargon, one paragraph screamed out for attention. 'It is, of course, obvious but nonetheless worth pointing out that many of these pictures still have substantial revenues forthcoming from ancillary markets which continue to accrue to Jeffrey's benefit ... Of course, these will continue 'forever' in the sense that even if he should leave one day there would be an arbitrated amount as to future income from the pictures.'

Jeffrey Katzenberg left the company in the most bitter circumstances in 1994 and claimed $580m in compensation based on the future earning power of the box office favourites with which he was associated. The agreement that Katzenberg should receive 2% of the profits from all his projects started under his command was written into his first contract in 1984.

At the time, Disney was in financial trouble. The company had narrowly escaped the clutches of raiders such as Saul Steinberg and Ivan Boesky. Each was bent on taking control and selling the company's assets including an unmatched collection of animated feature films going back to *Steamboat Willie*. Katzenberg's bonus clause was a mighty, if initially valueless, incentive. As Eisner was later to claim in a court deposition, neither contract 'anticipated this bonus provision to be meaningful ... we knew there were going to be big, big deficits.' 'In 1984,' he said, 'we were all quite confident there would be no profits to share.' However, in the following 10 years, Katzenberg was to earn $100m in cash compensation alone. More than 20% came from his share of profits.

Throughout this period, the two men appeared to complement each other. Eisner was the instinctive operator with the ability to detect successful shows and films, while Katzenberg (known for his inexhaustible energy) was the irrepressible studio boss who succeeded because he was 'focused, driven and relentless'. Second-in-command to Mr Eisner was Frank Wells, the group president, but he died in a helicopter crash in 1994, and two days later, Katzenberg demanded his job – one he had wanted for six years. When he was refused the job, Katzenberg stormed out to set up a rival entertainment company, DreamWorks, with Stephen Spielberg and music billionaire, David Geffen.

Disney's central argument in the case against Katzenberg was that the plaintiff had made a 'seat-of-the-pants' guess about the future earning power of his output as studio boss. In his first four years, by Eisner's own account, 31 of the 35 live action films from Walt Disney studios made a profit. In 1993, when Katzenberg was in virtual sole control of the studio (his 'genius' era) only 10 of his 26 live action productions made money, and the studio lost $36m. The 76 non-animation films made in his second four years earned $62m, compared with $200m from 35 in his 'pre-genius' era.

According to the company, the gross future earning power of the 1,000 projects started by Katzenberg is $7bn. This would entitle him to $140m, not the $580m he now demands. Discounted in accordance with a settlement formula agreed in the first stage of the court hearings, Mr Katzenberg – who has already received about $100m in part settlement – would get virtually nothing more if Disney's arguments prevail. Everything turned on the valuation of Disney's feature animation productions.

The widely publicised courtroom dispute between Katzenberg and Disney was settled in July 1999 by Disney granting an undisclosed amount of money to the plaintiff. Disney preferred to pay, rather than go into details about its future plans for expansion into China. Both sides claim to have won the battle – but both continue to face serious business problems.

Income from Katzenberg Disney projects 1988-94 ($m)		
Product	Release	Operating income ($m)
The Lion King	1994	810
Aladdin	1993	687
Beauty and the Beast	1992	409
The Little Mermaid	1990	279
Toy Story	1996	276
Home Improvement	1992	264
Pocahontas	1995	255
Pretty Woman	1990	136
Sister Act	1992	124
New Winnie the Pooh	1988	121
SUB TOTAL		3,360
All other Katzenberg projects		312
TOTAL		**$3,672**

FINANCIAL TIMES
World business newspaper.

Legal brief

A contract is an agreement between two parties or more to create legal obligations between them, usually in writing, and following basic conditions:

a) that an offer made by one party should be accepted by the other;

b) that there is a consideration, which is the price paid by one person in exchange for the other person promising to do something;

c) that there is an intention to create legal relations.

Vocabulary tasks

A Word search

Find a word or phrase in the text that has a similar meaning.

1 complicated language associated with specialised subjects (para 2)
   j.argon...........

2 large amount of income (para 2)
   s................... r...................

3 additional or extra markets which lead to sources of income (para 2)
   a...................

4 when money due to be paid to someone grows over time (para 2)
   a...................

5 sum of money, established by a court, that someone is owed (para 2)
   a................... a...................

6 money paid to someone because they have been hurt (para 3)
   c...................

7 part of a contract offering a percentage of company profits (para 4)
   b................... c...................

8 statement made to the court (para 4)
   d...................

9 financial losses (para 4)
   d...................

10 someone who brings a legal action against someone in a court of law (para 6)
   p...................

B Style

These phrases (**1–10**) are used in the text for effect. Match them with the definitions.

1 slanting across (line 6)
2 screamed out for attention (line 19)
3 in the most bitter circumstances (line 32)
4 escaped the clutches of (line 45)
5 raiders (line 46)
6 bent on taking control (line 47)
7 mighty (line 53)
8 stormed out (line 84)
9 seat-of-the-pants guess (line 91)
10 by his own account (line 94)

a) powerful
b) at an angle
c) left quickly, in an angry way
d) a rough estimate, not carefully calculated
e) determined to be the boss
f) aggressive business operators
g) according to him, in his words
h) demanded to be treated seriously
i) in a very angry and upsetting situation
j) avoiding being captured by

C Phrases with *contract*

Use an appropriate form of the words in the box to complete each sentence.

| draft | draw up | sign | break | renew | void | bid for | exchange |

1 Six specialist lawyers were asked to ......*draft*........ the contract with the Chinese consortium.

2 Jeffrey Katzenberg .... his contract with Disney in 1988.

3 The collaboration was a great success, so they were happy to .... the contract.

4 Finally, all parties agreed on all the clauses and provisions and .... the contract.

5 There was an official competition for companies to construct the new railway – each had to .... the contract.

6 The judge said that the actress had left the film-set without finishing the film, and thus had .... her contract.

7 Both parties failed to keep the conditions of the deal so the contract was ....

8 The buyer of the house and the seller of the house .... contracts after a successful negotiation on the price and removal date.

Over to you

1 Imagine you have a fixed contract of 35 hours a week to work, but your employer expects you to work overtime nearly every week. Complain! Prepare a set of notes you could refer to whilst holding a face-to-face conversation, or make notes that you could include in the letter you might write. Good lawyers always prepare for interviews or meetings!

2 Imagine you have bought something from a friend but the item is faulty when you try to use it. Compose a letter explaining the problem, and what you think your friend should do.

Civil litigation

Discuss these questions.

1 Do you think that public interest should come before private loyalty?

2 When an employee feels their company is acting in a dangerous or irresponsible way and they tell the world about it, it is called *whistle-blowing*. Is'whistle-blowing an ethical or a legal matter, in your opinion?

A Understanding main points

Read the text on the opposite page about a case of civil litigation and answer these questions.

1 What kind of product does British Biotech make?

2 Did they stand to profit if the new drugs were successful?

3 Why was the US Securities and Exchange Commission worried about Biotech?

4 Do you think Biotech's share price increased or decreased after the first press release about marimastat?

5 What position did Dr Millar hold when he worked for British Biotech?

6 What reason did the company give for dismissing Dr Millar?

B How the text is organised

What do these underlined words refer to in the text?

1 its directors (line 2)   *British Biotech*

2 patients taking their drug (line 23)

3 this has been prompted (line 31)

4 which would allow them (line 43)

5 warned them of his fears (line 55)

6 these moves (line 66)

7 no case for it to answer (line 78)

Brit Biotech directors could face US lawsuits over marimastat claims

By Jonathan Guthrie

British Biotech confirmed that one or more of its directors could face civil lawsuits in the US, brought by the Securities and Exchange Commission. The markets watchdog has been investigating whether press releases issued in 1995 and 1996 were over-optimistic about the prospects for the anti-cancer drug marimastat. A spokesman for Biotech said that the advice received from their lawyers was that there was no basis for the case, because the company had not violated any US securities laws.

It was understood by Biotech that the SEC's concerns were based on claims made on the use of cancer antigens[1]. At least one company release reported that the rate of antigen production had fallen in patients taking their drug, marimastat, suggesting the treatment was effective.

Dr Andrew Millar was sacked as head of clinical research at British Biotech. He had claimed that the trials of the drug had become a matter of public interest following extensive media coverage. This had been prompted by his campaign to oust the British Biotech chief executive and change the strategy of the company.

Dr Millar became concerned about the company's over-optimism about the future of two drugs under trial, so he decided to take extreme measures by himself. He did not believe the drugs worked well enough to achieve regulatory approval, which would allow them to be launched commercially, and was concerned that the drugs were actually causing serious side-effects on the trial patients. He was also aware of negative assessments of the drug by the Danish Medicines Agency but Biotech issued a press release that the results were 'statistically significant'. He contacted one of the main investors supporting Biotech (Perpetual) and warned them of his fears. He hoped to stop the drugs being tested, and to reveal that they were far less promising than investors had been led to believe. He hoped that the shareholders of Biotech would change the strategy of ambitious expansion, envisioned by the Chief Executive.

The Chief Executive, hearing of these moves, suspended Dr Millar and a few weeks later, he was fired without compensation at a disciplinary meeting for 'revealing confidential information to third parties'. In announcing the sacking, British Biotech cited a confidential report prepared by Cameron McKenna, the law firm. The document proved, the company said, that directors' share dealings had complied with stock exchange rules, and there was no case for it to answer to the SEC. The company has threatened to take legal action against Dr Millar to prevent him disclosing information gained as an employee. He says jail – a possible consequence of breaking any injunction placed upon him – is a small price to pay for the freedom to speak out.

FINANCIAL TIMES
World business newspaper.

1 substances, often toxins, that can help the human body produce antibodies which fight disease

Legal brief

Employees who blow the whistle on their employers (expose illegal or dishonest practices) are protected by law in the US. If they are fired or otherwise penalised for whistle-blowing, they can sue. If the employee just complains to someone inside the company, that is not whistle-blowing. They must report their concerns to someone outside the company, who works for the government or a law enforcement agency.

Vocabulary tasks

A Word search

Find a word or phrase in the text that has a similar meaning.

1 break US law regarding stocks and shares (para 1)

v.*iolate*........... US s.*ecurities*....... l.*aws*..............

2 lost his job (para 3)

s....................

3 after the press had become very interested in the case (para 3)

f.................. e.................... m.................... c...................

4 attempt to remove the boss (para 3)

c.................. to o.................. the c.................. e..................

5 get official clearance to produce the drug (para 4)

a.................. r.................... a..................

6 when drugs make some patients very ill (para 4)

c.................. s.................... s...................-e..................

7 criticism of the drug (para 4)

n.................. a..................

8 removed from a job with no financial reward (para 5)

f.................. without c..................

B On your behalf

Match the individuals and institutions with their descriptions.

1 Securities and Exchange Commission
2 company lawyers
3 spokesperson
4 Danish Medicines Agency
5 media
6 whistle-blowers
7 regulators

a) newspapers, magazines, radio and TV companies
b) people responsible for the lawful and proper conduct of an industry
c) organisation supervising the US stock market
d) professional organisation qualified to assess pharmaceutical research in Denmark
e) people who expose wrongdoing in the institutions in which they work
f) person who speaks to the press on behalf of a company, organisation or family
g) solicitors employed by business organisations

Over to you

1 Think of examples of whistle-blowing by private or government workers that you have heard about. What was their employer doing that made them blow the whistle? Who did they tell?

2 You have heard your boss explaining very confidential matters to someone on the phone about plans your company has for a major investment. You suspect he is leaking information to someone outside the company. Write a letter to the managing director setting out your concerns and asking her for advice on how to proceed.

1 Discuss these questions.

a) Do you live in a country where the seasons are very different? Think of the countries where the seasons are most extreme.

b) Do you eat fruit out of season? What kind of fruit?

c) Where does fruit imported into your country usually come from?

d) Do food products arrive by air, sea or road? How many days do you think they are in transit?

2 Match these terms with their definitions. Use a dictionary to help you if necessary.

1 civil	**a)**	place where you live
2 tort	**b)**	company responsible for transporting goods
3 attempt to sue	**c)**	not regarded as part of criminal law
4 jurisdiction	**d)**	legal power to make decisions
5 carrier	**e)**	as understood or meant by the law
6 insurer	**f)**	try to bring a legal case against
7 derogation	**g)**	breach of civil law which requires compensation
8 contractual relationship	**h)**	the insurance company who sold the policy
9 domicile	**i)**	relationship as defined in the contract
10 within the meaning of the convention	**j)**	not following the rules or doing your duty

A Understanding main points

Read the text on the opposite page about a cargo of spoiled fruit and answer the questions.

1 How many insurance companies are involved in the lawsuit?   *nine*

2 What was the name of the company that received the damaged pears?

3 How many different parties are they suing?

4 What was the nationality of the company that exported the pears?

5 What happened to the pears?

6 Was there any dispute about the condition of the pears?

7 Why did the European Court of Justice rule that the action against the Dutch carrier and its master was not a 'matter relating to contract'?

Ruling says where the rot sets in

European court

An action brought by the buyer of a damaged consignment of fruit against the carrier of the goods was not an action for breach of contract but an action for negligence or tort within the meaning of the Brussels Convention, the European Court of Justice ruled recently.

The case arose out of proceedings brought by nine insurance companies led by Reunion Europeenne over a damaged cargo of pears from Australia received by the insured, Brambi Fruits, a French company. The insurers attempted to sue the Australian company which issued the bill of lading, the Dutch company which carried the fruit (although it was not named in the bill of lading), and the master of the ship. The fruit had ripened prematurely because the ship's cooling system had failed.

The French court said it had jurisdiction in respect of the Australian shipper but declined jurisdiction over the Dutch carrier and the master. The Paris Court of Appeal confirmed that decision, but the Court of Cassation stayed proceedings pending a ruling from Luxembourg on the Brussels convention which covers jurisdiction and the recognition and enforcement of civil and commercial judgments in the European Union.

The Dutch carrier and the master argued that the dispute was 'a matter relating to a contract' under the convention because it was based on the bill of lading.

The Court said that the phrase was to be interpreted independently and could not be taken to refer to how the legal relationship in question was classified by the relevant national law.

Under the convention, the general principle was that the courts of the state in which the defendant was domiciled would have jurisdiction and it was only by way of derogation from that principle in certain cases that a defendant might or must be sued elsewhere.

The Court said the bill of lading did not disclose any contractual relationship between Brambi and the Dutch carrier and the master. The action against them was not therefore a 'matter relating to a contract' within the meaning of the convention. However the action was a matter relating to tort within the meaning of the convention. Therefore the carrier and the master could be sued in the courts of either the place where the damage occurred or the place where the event giving rise to the damage occurred.

In cases such as this involving international transport, the place where the damage occurred could only be the place where the carrier was to deliver the goods, it said. Accordingly, the place where the buyer merely discovered the existence of the damage could not serve to determine the place where the harmful event occurred within the meaning of the convention.

FINANCIAL TIMES
World business newspaper.

Legal brief

In this international dispute, the Court ruled that the case should be heard where the damage was discovered, in France, where the fruit was delivered. The Court also ruled that the case was not about contract law, but was a tort, technically another branch of the law.

A tort: the object of proceedings in tort is not punishment but compensation or reparation to the plaintiff for the loss or injury caused by the defendant. It is therefore a matter of civil law.

Breach of contract: in contract the duties are fixed by the parties themselves, who impose terms and conditions themselves by their agreement. In tort, on the other hand, the duties are fixed by law (common or statute).

B Different cases, different courts

Match the description of each court with its function.

1 A magistrates court (UK)   *b*
2 The Court of Cassation (France)
3 The Supreme Court (USA)
4 The High Court of Justice (UK)

5 The European Court of Justice
6 Court of Appeal (Civil Division) (UK)
7 The Crown Court (UK)

a) The Court is composed of The Lord Chancellor, the Lord Chief Justice, the Master of the Rolls, the President of the Family Division and 28 other Lords Justice of Appeal and may uphold, amend or reverse the decision of a lower court or order a new trial.

b) There are 900 of them, dealing mostly with cases of criminal law and common law and preserving the local peace. They are presided over by Justices of the Peace (or magistrates).

c) It consists of three divisions: the Queen's Bench Division, the Chancery Division and the Family Division. It deals with civil cases.

e) It deals with all the criminal cases passed to it from the Magistrates Court and has jurisdiction over all serious offences. It is presided over by High Court or circuit judges and always uses a jury.

f) In France this is the final court of appeal.

g) In the US, this is the highest court in the country.

h) In Europe, this court overrules any other civil court in any member state.

Vocabulary tasks

A Word search

Find a word or phrase in the text that has a similar meaning.

1 lawsuit (para 1)
   a.*ction*...........

2 goods spoiled in transit (para 1)
   d................... c...................

3 breaking of the agreement signed by both parties (para 1)
   b................... of c...................

4 document listing the goods loaded before transportation (para 2)
   b................... of l...................

5 said it was not within the legal power of the court (para 3)
   d................... j...................

6 agreed with that judgment (para 3)
   c................... the d...................

7 postponed the case (para 3)
   s................... p...................

8 waiting for (para 3)

p....................

9 putting the law into action (para 3)

e..................

10 decisions in business cases (para 3)

c.................... j....................

B Partners

Contracts involve at least two parties. Find the partners in these relationships.

1 buyer   **a)** defendant

2 plaintiff   **b)** seller

3 offer   **c)** follower

4 leader   **d)** loser

5 doctor   **e)** patient

6 lawyer   **f)** client

7 prosecution   **g)** acceptance

8 winner   **h)** defence

Over to you

1 Imagine you are a buyer of fruit for a large restaurant. The last order you received was rotten and you lost business as a result. After leaving several messages on the phone, a week has passed without any apology or explanation from the supplier. You decide to write a letter of complaint. What details should you include in your letter? What proof can you offer that the fruit was rotten?

2 Work with a partner.

A: You are the buyer. You have not had a reply to your calls and letter for over two weeks. Visit the warehouse and ask to speak to the manager. Explain your story. Threaten to tell your story to the press.

B: You are the manager. This is the first time you have heard about this complaint. You know nothing about a letter. Try to make the customer realise that you need to have proof. Ask for some evidence. Warn A that if they libel the firm, you are prepared to take legal action. But if there is a genuine grievance, of course you will try to make up for the loss. But you need evidence.

Who's to blame?

Discuss these questions.

1 Have you ever found yourself in conflict with elected officials or a local authority?

2 Suppose your street lights did not work and you injured yourself one night as you were walking home. Who would you blame for the injury?

A Understanding main points

Read the text on the opposite page about liability for an accident and answer these questions.

1 Who brought the lawsuit against the State of North Carolina Department of Labor for the failure of the State to ensure safe factory conditions?

2 Where did the fire take place?

3 Who is appealing against the decision that the North Carolina Department of Labor and its Occupational Safety and Health Division were guilty of negligence?

4 Which Act is the basis for the lawsuit complaint?

5 Why were so many employees hurt or killed in the fire?

6 How many safety violations did the investigation reveal after the fire?

7 Does the ruling by the Supreme Court mean that the State is immune from liability in this case?

B Understanding expressions

Choose the best explanation for each of these words or phrases from the text.

1 imposed a duty (line 24)

   a) obliged someone to pay tax

   b) made something someone's responsibility

2 breach of duty (line 27)

   a) breaking your word

   b) not doing your official job properly

3 limited and obscure concept (line 83)

   a) idea that people do not understand

   b) notion designed for a very rare situation

4 eviscerate the Tort Claims Act (line 90)

   a) change the meaning of the Act

   b) remove an important part of the Act

Department of Labor, Occupational Safety and Health Division

No. 81PA97 (filed 6 February 1998)

Plaintiffs commenced this negligence action against defendants, the North Carolina Department of Labor and its Occupational Safety and Health Division, pursuant to the Tort Claims Act. Plaintiffs sought damages for injuries or deaths resulting from a fire at the Imperial Foods Products plant in Hamlet, North Carolina. Defendants moved, pursuant to North Carolina Government Statutes Rules 12(b) (1), (2) and (6), to dismiss plaintiffs' claims. Deputy Commissioner denied the motions. The full Commission affirmed and adopted his decision.

The Court of Appeal agreed that the State had been negligent. It held that North Carolina Government Statutes, which describes the authority, power, and duties of the Commissioner of Labor, imposed a duty upon the defendants to inspect the workplaces of North Carolina and that the breach of this duty gave rise to the plaintiffs' action for negligence. It further held that the 'public duty doctrine' did not apply to actions brought against the State under the Tort Claims Act. On 5 June 1997 the Supreme Court granted the State of North Carolina (the defendants) the right to petition them to re-examine the Appeal Court's decision. This is called a 'discretionary review'.

The Supreme Court Judges accepted the facts, as presented to the court by the plaintiffs, as factually correct. On 3 September 1991 a fire started in a section of a chicken-processing factory belonging to Imperial Foods Products in Hamlet, North Carolina. The fire grew in intensity and spread rapidly. Plaintiffs were either former employees of Imperial Foods who suffered injury in the fire or personal representatives of the estates of employees who died in the fire. They were lawfully inside the factory at the time of the fire. They could not easily escape the plant or the fire because the exits in the plant were unmarked, blocked and inaccessible. It was only after the fire had taken place that the North Carolina Health Department conducted their first and only inspection in the plant's 11 year history of operation. As a result of this inspection, numerous violations of the Safety Act, including the plant's inadequate and blocked fire-suppression system, were discovered. Eighty-three citations against Imperial Foods Products for violations of safety and health standards were issued.

The majority of the appeal judges of the Supreme Court decided that the State of North Carolina was not negligent in its duty to carry out fire and safety inspections, on a legal technicality. One of the judges disagreed very strongly.

The dissenting judge, Justice Orr, said:

'The majority opinion erroneously takes a limited and obscure common law concept, the public duty doctrine, which has traditionally applied only to municipalities and their law enforcement responsibilities, and expands the doctrine's application to effectively eviscerate the Tort Claims Act. As a result, the right of individuals to sue the State for negligent acts committed by the State, a right expressly conveyed by the General Assembly, is nullified without the support of any precedential authority permitting such an indulgence.'

From *www.aoc.state.nc.us*, North Carolina Administritive Office of the Courts

5 expressly conveyed (line 94)

   a) specifically granted

   b) transported very fast

6 a right is nullified (line 94)

   a) the case has to start again

   b) a right is cancelled and withdrawn

Legal brief

This case was controversial because there was a disagreement between the lower courts and the Supreme Court. The final word was the majority opinion of the Supreme Court, which said the State of North Carolina was not liable to pay compensation to the fire victims on a technical point which makes it impossible for a private citizen to sue a government organisation.

Federal Tort Claims Act: the government of the United States may not be sued in tort – civil wrong-doing – without its consent. However, in 1946 that consent was granted and the Act set out the conditions for suits and claims against the federal government.

Vocabulary tasks

A Key terms

Match these legal terms (**1–17**) with their definitions.

Paragraph 1

1	negligence action	**a)**	in accordance with
2	pursuant to	**b)**	lawsuit about failing to do a duty
3	move to dismiss plaintiffs' claims	**c)**	agreed with
4	deny the motions	**d)**	apply for a ruling against the plaintiffs
5	affirmed and adopted	**e)**	refuse to accept the arguments as valid

Paragraph 2

6	hold	**f)**	give the entitlement to seek further court decisions
7	impose a duty	**g)**	according to the Tort Claims Act
8	under the Tort Claims Act	**h)**	express the opinion
9	grant the right to petition	**i)**	oblige them to act in a certain way

Paragraphs 3 and 4

10	estates of the employees	**j)**	factory
11	lawfully	**k)**	families of the dead employees
12	plant	**l)**	detailed interpretation of the law
13	legal technicality	**m)**	not illegally

Paragraph 5

14	erroneously	**n)**	guided by previous decisions and precedents
15	expand the application	**o)**	widen the law to refer to cases not originally intended
16	precedential	**p)**	governed by personal preference, not legal authority
17	indulgence	**q)**	incorrectly

B Verbs of agreeing and disagreeing

1 Write these words in the appropriate columns.

concur dismiss the motion share the opinion affirm adopt the decision treat as true reverse a decision dismiss claims dissent assent

agree   disagree

................*concur*.....................   ....

....

....

....

....

....

2 What do you think the expression *agree to differ* means?

C Complete the sentence

Use an appropriate word or phrase from Exercise B to complete each sentence.

1 On the basis of the evidence I have studied, I have to .....*agree*...... with the court's ruling.

2 Both of us .... that the fire was started by accident.

3 The High Court completely disagreed with the lower court on appeal, and ....

4 The full Commission .... and .... his decision yesterday.

5 The defendants asked the court to .... the plaintiff's ....

6 I cannot .... to that. I do not believe it is the correct course of action to follow.

D Definitions

Match these terms with their definitions.

1 commenced   **a)** also agreed

2 sought damages   **b)** began

3 pursuant to   **c)** caused

4 further held   **d)** following, in accordance with

5 gave rise to   **e)** asked for financial compensation

6 granted a petition   **f)** allowed an appeal for a legal review

Over to you

1 Write a simple summary of the Federal Tort case and the Supreme Court's decision, and why Judge Orr dissented.

2 List the minimum safety measures you think a factory should have. Decide what duties the management should have, and what protection should be provided by state law.

Business lawyers

Before you read

Discuss these questions.

1 In your country, are there different kinds of lawyers? If so, what are the differences?

2 Can you describe the normal way that lawyers become qualified to practise law in your country?

Reading tasks

A Understanding main points

Mark these statements T (true) or F (false), according to the information in the text on the opposite page. Find the part of the text that gives the correct information.

1 If you have any kind of legal question the first person you consult is a barrister.   F

2 A barrister and a solicitor are both qualified lawyers in the UK.

3 'Preparing a brief for counsel' means a solicitor writes a detailed description of a case so as to inform the expert (the barrister) of all the facts and main legal points.

4 A solicitor cannot speak in a higher court.

5 A barrister in the UK is an independent qualified lawyer.

6 If you want to work for a law firm and receive a regular salary, you should become a solicitor.

7 There are more solicitors than barristers.

8 Barristers often specialise in particular areas of the law, like property or contracts.

9 A barrister may become a judge, but a solicitor cannot.

10 The law is the same in England as in Scotland but differs in Wales.

11 A Recorder is a part-time judge.

12 One of the roles of the police in the UK is to assemble sufficient evidence for a criminal case to come to court.

B Understanding expressions

Choose the best explanation for each of these words or phrases from the text.

1 tenders advice (line 4)

   a) offers advice

   b) bids for advice

   c) refuses advice

2 briefing solicitor (line 6)

   a) lawyer who works quickly

   b) lawyer who writes a letter

   c) lawyer who prepares a case for court

Solicitor or barrister?

The solicitor is the first point of contact with the law for a client in the UK. The solicitor listens carefully to the client, making sure their needs are clearly understood and then explains the legal position and tenders 5 advice. By contrast, barristers will only see the client in the company of a briefing solicitor. The barrister is the specialist with particular skills in advocacy, a consultant who will examine the case and decide what line to take in court. The barrister will be reliant on 10 the detailed brief prepared by the client's solicitor. There are only a few solicitors who are allowed to present cases in the higher courts. Many more solicitors work in their litigation departments and spend much of their time preparing briefs for counsel. Barristers 15 are self-employed in the independent Bar. Solicitors are normally salaried and may be offered a share in the profits of the practice if they are successful.

The Bar is a small but influential independent body with just over 8,000 practising barristers in over 400 20 chambers in England and Wales. In addition, there are about 2,000 barristers employed as in-house lawyers.

The Bar is an advocacy profession. The Bar's right of audience in the higher courts remains virtually unchallenged. The work divides equally between civil 25 and criminal law. There are over 70 specialist areas, including major ones like chancery (mainly property and finance) and the commercial bar.

Judges in England and Wales have mostly been barristers of 10 years' standing, then Queen's Counsellors, 30 and are appointed by the Lord Chancellor. Judges cannot work as barristers once they are appointed. A barrister who is a part-time judge is known as a Recorder. The Crown Prosecutor, who works for the Director of Public Prosecutions, is responsible for prosecuting 35 criminals based on evidence presented by the police.

Solicitors do a variety of work – corporate and commercial, litigation, property, private law, banking and project finance, employment law and environmental law. There are about 66,000 practising solicitors in England and Wales.

From *Career Scope*, Autumn 1997

3 advocacy (line 7)

  a) speaking or pleading in the court

  b) lawyers

  c) rich and famous people

4 line (line 9)

  a) queue

  b) time to allocate

  c) position

5 salaried (line 16)

  a) with postgraduate degrees

  b) receiving regular pay

  c) independent

6 practising (line 19)

  a) not very good yet

  b) in training

  c) professionally working

7 chambers (line 20)

  a) bedrooms

  b) barristers' offices

  c) changing rooms

8 in-house (line 21)

  a) hoteliers

  b) employed by a company

  c) independent

9 right of audience (line 22)

  a) performing on stage

  b) tickets to observe

  c) allowed to speak in court

10 commercial bar (line 27)

  a) expensive drinks

  b) law of business

  c) trade and industry ban

C Comparing texts

Read the text below and complete the sentences which follow.

Attorney at Law

A person admitted to practise law in their respective state and authorised to perform both civil and criminal legal functions for clients, including drafting of legal documents, giving of legal advice, and representing such before courts, administrative agencies, boards, etc.

Prosecutor

One who prosecutes another for a crime in the name of the government. One who instigates the prosecution upon which an accused is arrested or who prefers an accusation against the party whom they suspect to be guilty, as does a district, county, or state's attorney on behalf of the state, or a United States Attorney for a federal district on behalf of the US government.

In **Spain**, the universities are in charge of the education of lawyers. Anyone completing a law degree is entitled to be called a lawyer and may work as a lawyer for a legal practice or in a company. However, to achieve public office and work for the State Judiciary, as a notary or judge, for example, graduate lawyers must compete for places through public examinations and then attend judicial school for two years. They then may be appointed as civil servants anywhere in the country.

1 In England and Wales, a ... *solicitor* ..... prepares briefs but does not represent the clients in court. This is done by a .... In the US, both functions are performed by an ....

2 In the US a .... instigates a prosecution against someone suspected of a crime. This can be done at district, county, state or federal level. In England and Wales this is done by the .... who works for the Department of Public Prosecutions.

3 In England and Wales, a judge is appointed by the Lord Chancellor from barristers who have worked successfully for over 10 years and who have attained the status of .... In Spain, lawyers wishing to become judges have to attend .... for .... years.

Vocabulary tasks

A Collocations

Match the verbs and nouns. Use a dictionary to help you if necessary.

1	instigate	**a)**	a client
2	bring	**b)**	a prosecution
3	prefer	**c)**	a copyright
4	prepare	**d)**	a suspect
5	reach	**e)**	a fee
6	settle	**f)**	out of court
7	charge	**g)**	a verdict
8	arrest	**h)**	a case
9	defend	**i)**	a brief
10	infringe	**j)**	an accusation

B Complete the sentences

Use an appropriate phrase from Exercise A to complete each sentence.

1 A prosecutor can ......*prefer*...... an ..*accusation*.. or .... a .... against someone suspected of committing a crime.

2 In the UK, only the Crown Prosecution Service can .... a .... against someone on a criminal charge.

3 By copying my novel and selling it as your own, you have not only .... my .... but also betrayed my trust as a friend.

4 The two sets of lawyers agreed not to go to trial but to .... out of ....

5 Some lawyers do not .... a .... if the client asks for very simple advice.

6 The jury took three days to .... a ....

7 All lawyers must .... their .... even if they doubt their innocence.

8 As a solicitor in a large company, I spend a lot of time .... for barristers.

9 The police had sufficient evidence of his guilt to .... the ....

C Branches of the law

Match the different branches of the law with the examples.

1	litigation	**a)**	treaties and cross-border agreements
2	corporate and commercial	**b)**	bringing lawsuits against others
3	family	**c)**	contracts and mergers
4	environmental	**d)**	rules applyied to how a prosecution or civil action is conducted
5	employment	**e)**	civil cases
6	private	**f)**	pleading a case in court on behalf of a client
7	advocacy	**g)**	divorce and marriage settlements
8	public international	**h)**	relating to creativity, published ideas and art forms
9	intellectual property	**i)**	equal opportunities and fair pay
10	procedural law	**j)**	regarding industrial waste and pollution

Over to you

1 Being a lawyer is regarded as one of the best professions in many countries. Think about what the different areas of specialisation are, and which you would choose, or have chosen, and why. Make notes under the headings: choice of specialisation; number of years of training; income expectations; responsibilities; kinds of clients; need for foreign languages; likely challenges and opportunities. Add any other points that occur to you.

2 Imagine you are a family solicitor. Give advice to someone who asks your professional opinion about a financial matter. Your client has asked you whether she should invest money she has inherited in the stock market or place it in the bank. Explain that you feel she should consult a financial expert first. Invite her to discuss any tax implications with her tax adviser.

18 | Inheritance tax and the family company

Before you read

Discuss these questions.

1 Have you ever played with Lego? Do you know in which European country Lego is made?
2 Can you describe the difference between a family-owned company and a publicly-owned company?
3 In your country, are taxes payable on the death of the owner of a company or head of a family?

Reading tasks

A Understanding main points

Read the text on the opposite page about the Danish Lego group and answer these questions.

1 Who owns the capital in Lego?
2 What does the present owner of Lego fear will happen to the company financially when he dies?
3 How is the company in Switzerland that controls Lego defined?
4 Under the new tax system, would an inheritor have to pay tax on the value of a company based in a country with higher taxes than Denmark?
5 Which country has the highest tax-to-GDP ratio, according to the text?
6 What change in Danish tax legislation has affected this company?
7 What would Lego do with the money if they did not have to pay the tax?
8 How is the new inheritance tax going to affect other major Danish family-owned companies, according to the text?

B Understanding details

Answer these questions.

1 When did the inheritance law in Denmark change?
2 What plans might not be carried out by the children of the owner?
3 When the owner of Lego dies, who does he think will buy his company?
4 Are all the Lego companies registered in Denmark?
5 Which ratio is named as being higher in Denmark than in Switzerland?
6 How much tax will the Lego inheritors have to pay?
7 Is Lego the only company in Denmark to have to pay this kind of tax?
8 Is the holding company in Switzerland bigger or smaller than the Danish holding company in terms of annual turnover?

Lego warns on change in law

Family status of Danish group threatened by changes to inheritance tax

By Hilary Barnes in Copenhagen

The owner of Lego has warned the Danish government that the future of the family-owned international toys group was in doubt 5 because of the country's inheritance tax regime. Kjeld Kirk Kristiansen, 50, said recent changes in legislation meant that when the next generation of the 10 family moved into Lego management, more than DKr3bn ($437m) would have to be taken out of the company to pay inheritance taxes. In letters to Mr Ole Stavad, the tax 15 minister, he said: 'Our plans to keep Lego as a family-owned Danish company cannot be carried out.'

In the letter, published in 20 *Borsen*, the business daily, Mr Kristiansen stopped short of saying a sale to foreign interests might be necessary if the legislation was not changed before he 25 died. However, Peter Ambeck Madsen, Lego's information manager, said: 'This is an obvious risk.' The threat to family control arises from the fact that part of the Lego 30 group is controlled through a holding company in Switzerland. This company is defined under the legislation as a finance company. In the case of a finance company 35 domiciled in a country where taxes are significantly lower than in Denmark (which has the highest tax-to-GDP[1] ratio in Europe after Sweden), a Danish inheritor will

The Lego Supercar

40 have to pay a differential tax on the capital value of the company.

Previously, the owner would only have been liable to pay tax if he or she sold the shares and 45 realised a capital gain. It is principally as a consequence of this change to previous legislation that Lego's owners will have to pay 'an additional' DKr3bn in inheritance 50 taxes. '[This is] money which can only be taken out of the business, where in my opinion it should rather be used for investment and jobs,' Mr Kristiansen told Mr 55 Stavad.

He argues that the company's corporate structure was set up for business, not tax avoidance, reasons. The Swiss holding company,

60 Interlego AG, was established in 1962. Lego seems to be unique in being caught by the legislation. 'I can't think of any other major company which will be caught,' 65 said Mr Ned Shelton, of Shelton International, a Copenhagen tax consultancy firm. Lego only publishes figures for the companies controlled through the Danish 70 holding company. This group of companies has an annual turnover of about DKr76bn and employs 9,800. The companies controlled from Switzerland have about 3,000 75 employees and turnover of about DKr2bn.

FINANCIAL TIMES
World business newspaper.

1 an abbreviation of Gross Domestic Product, the total revenues earned by a country from its goods and services in a year

Legal brief

Each country has its own tax regime. In Europe, most countries insist that citizens who keep wealth outside the territory where they live have to pay tax on it, sooner or later. The phrase *death duties* in the UK means the same as *inheritance tax* in Denmark – that is, tax paid by the heirs to an estate on the wealth and property they inherit.

Vocabulary tasks

A Describing company structures

Use an appropriate word or phrase from the box to complete each sentence.

> companies capital company corporate domiciled
> holding inherit inheritance tax inheritor shares

1 The Lego group is made up of several ..*companies*....

2 When the owner dies, his children will .... the firm.

3 At the moment, it looks as though they will have to pay a huge amount of money in ....

4 Any .... that is set up in another, lower tax country, is subject to this.

5 The Danish law says that any finance firm .... abroad must pay differential tax.

6 The .... structure of Lego was designed for business reasons, not taxation reasons.

7 Part of the Lego company is controlled through a .... company abroad.

8 The person who receives money from someone who dies is the ....

9 The Danish inheritor will pay tax on the .... value of the company.

10 The equity or ownership of a family company or public company is divided into ....
which can be bought or sold.

B Collocations

Match these nouns as they occur in the text.

1 capital   a) taxes
2 inheritance   b) gain
3 information   c) avoidance
4 family   d) structure
5 holding   e) manager
6 capital   f) control
7 corporate   g) value
8 tax   h) company

C Prepositions

Complete these sentences with an appropriate preposition.

1 The future ......*of*......... the firm is ......*in*.......... doubt.

2 The owners will have to pay tax .... their inheritance.

3 Companies set .... in foreign countries often pay lower local tax.

4 The firm may be bought .... foreign interests.

5 The ownership will pass .... the hands of foreigners.

6 Inherited money is passed .... from one generation .... another.

7 A new president will have to take ....

8 The money should be used .... investment, not .... taxation.

9 According .... a spokesman, there is a danger .... the company being sold.

10 The owner is worried .... what will happen to the company when he dies.

D Verbs for gaining control

Match these verbs and the nouns. Use a dictionary to help you if necessary.

1	make	a)	race
2	make	b)	a rival bid
3	win the	c)	the helm
4	gain	d)	a stake
5	acquire	e)	over
6	take	f)	the company
7	head	g)	global forces
8	maintain	h)	control
9	adapt to	i)	an offer
10	take	j)	a majority shareholding

Over to you

1 On the evidence of the text, the future of family firms seems to be at risk. Is it possible for successful family-owned companies to survive into the next century if they must pay out large sums of money in inheritance tax to the government? Why does it seem important to some people to preserve family-owned firms like Lego and Fiat? Think about the economic, social and financial problems for the family, and how they may overcome them, and the advantages and dangers of relocating businesses to 'friendlier' tax authorities.

2 Do you know the law in your country regarding death duties or inheritance tax? A will is a legal document that explains who the owner wants to leave their wealth to. What happens in your country if someone dies without making a will?

Glossary

English	French	Spanish
accrue	revenir à	incrementar
advocacy	plaidoyer	abogacía
aiders and abettors	complices	cómplices
allege	alléguer	alegar
ancillary markets	marchés auxiliaires	mercados auxiliares
arbitration	arbitrage	arbitraje
arson	crime d'incendie volontaire	incendio provocado
bankrupt	en faillite	bancarrota
barrister	avocat	abogado
beneficiaries	bénéficiaires	beneficiarios
bias	opinion préconçue	prejuicio
bill of lading	connaissement	conocimiento de embarque
black economy	travail « au noir »	economía subterránea
block	bloquer	bloquear
bond	bon (du Trésor), signature	bono; garantía
bonus clause	clause relative aux primes	cláusula sobre primas
bulk cash	argent en vrac	grandes cantidades de dinero
burglary	cambriolage	allanamiento de morada
capital gain	plus-values	plusvalía
capital value	valeur en capital	valor en capital
capitalise	capitaliser	capitalizar
cargo	cargaison	cargamento
chambers	cabinets	cámaras
circuit court	cour itinérante	tribunal de distrito
circulation	diffusion	circulación
cite	citer	citar
civil	civil	civil
civil servant	fonctionnaire	funcionario público
claim rights to	faire valoir ses droits sur	reclamar los derechos a
code-sharing	partage de code	intercambio de códigos
commercial assets	actif commercial	capital comercial
commercial bar	tribunal de commerce	tribunal mercantil
compensation	dédommagement	compensación
complicity	complicité	complicidad
comply with	se conformer à	acatar
con artist	escroc	timador
conceal material facts	dissimuler des faits essentiels	ocultar hechos importantes
confer on	s'entretenir sur	conferir
confidentiality agreement	accord de confidentialité	acuerdo de confidencialidad
construe	interpréter, analyser	interpretar
contentious	contentieux	contencioso
contingent on	dépendant de, subordonné à	condicionado a
convicted	déclaré coupable, condamné	condenado
copyright	droit d'auteur	derechos de autor
counsel	conseil	organismo consultivo
counterfeiting	contrefaçon	falsificación
court	tribunal	tribunal
criminal	criminelle	criminal
damages	dommages-intérêts	daños
death duties	droits de succession	impuestos sobre sucesión
de-list	déréférencer	retirar de Bolsa

German	Polish
anwachsen	narastać, przypadać
Anwaltstätigkeit	adwokatura
Mittäter	współsprawcy przestępstwa
behaupten, vorbringen	twierdzić, imputować
Nebenmärkte	rynki wtórne
Schlichtung	arbitraż, sąd polubowny
Brandstiftung	podpalenie
bankrott	bankrut
Rechtsanwalt (bei oberen Gerichten)	adwokat (uprawniony do występowania przed sądem)
Nutznießer	beneficjent, spadkobierca
Parteilichkeit, Befangenheit	stronniczość, uprzedzenie
Konnossement	konosament
Schattenwirtschaft	czarna ekonomia
aufhalten, stoppen	blokować
Schuldverschreibungen, bindend	więź, oblig
Zulagenklausel	klauzula premiowa
große Bargeldbeträge	duża suma gotówki
Einbruch	włamanie
Veräußerungsgewinn	zysk kapitałowy
Kapitalwert	wartość kapitałowa
kapitalisieren	kapitalizować
Fracht, Kargo	ładunek
Anwaltskanzlei von Barristern	kancelaria adwokacka
Bezirksgericht	sąd objazdowy
Umlauf	nakład, obieg
zitieren	cytować, pozywać
zivil	obywatelski, świecki
Beamter	urzędnik państwowy
Rechte auf etwas geltend machen	żądać praw do
Gemeinschaftsflug	wspólne stosowanie kodów
Geschäftsguthaben	środki handlowe
Anwälte, die sich auf Handelsrecht spezialisiert haben	adwokatura handlowa
Entschädigung, Schadensersatz	odszkodowanie
Mittäterschaft	współudział
etwas einhalten/befolgen	stosować się do
Trickdieb	szarlatan
wichtige Tatsachen verschweigen/zurückhalten	zataić ważne fakty
verleihen, übertragen	naradzać się na temat
Vertraulichkeitsabkommen	umowa poufna
auslegen	interpretować, wyjaśniać
strittig	sporny, kłótliwy
abhängen von	uwarunkowany (czymś)
verurteilt	skazany
Urheberrecht	prawo autorskie
Anwalt	rada, radca prawny
fälschen	fałszerstwo
Gericht	sąd
kriminell	kryminalne
Schadensersatz	odszkodowanie
Erbschaftssteuer	podatek spadkowy
Börsenzulassung entziehen	usunięte z indeksu

deposition	témoignage en justice	declaración jurada
derogation from a principle	dérogation à un principe	desestimación de un principio
deter	dissuader	disuadir
diplomatic cover	immunité diplomatique	amparo diplomático
disburse	débourser, décaisser	desembolsar
disclosure	divulgation	divulgación
discrimination	discrimination	discriminación
dispute	différend, conflit, litige	disputa
disseminate	disséminer	divulgar
distortion	distorsion	distorsión
distributors (film)	distributeurs	distribuidores
doctrine	doctrine	doctrina
domiciled	domicilié	domiciliado
drug cartels	cartels de la drogue	carteles de drogas
due diligence	diligence normale	diligencia debida
egregious	extrême, monumentale	insigne
embezzled funds	fonds détournés	malversación de fondos
equal opportunities	égalité des chances	igualdad de oportunidades
evidence	preuve, les preuves	evidencia
eviscerate	éviscérer	desentrañar
fake	contrefaçon	falsificación
federal court	Cour Fédérale	tribunal federal
file suit	intenter un procès	demandar
fine	amende	multa
franchise	franchise	franquicia
fraud	fraude	fraude
grant custody	octroyer le droit de garde	conceder la custodia
grounds	fondement	motivos
hacker	pirate d'informatique	pirata informático
held illegal	tenu illégal, jugé illicite	retener ilegalmente
hereby	par les présentes	por el presente
hereinafter	ci-après	en adelante
hoax	canular	aviso falso
hold liable	rendre responsable	hacer responsable
holding company	holding	compañía matriz
ill-gotten money	fonds mal acquis	dinero negro
illegal	illégal, illicite	ilegal
illicit	illicite	ilícito
immunity	immunité	inmunidad
impliedly	tacitement	de manera implícita
indemnify	indemniser, dédommager	indemnizar
infiltration	infiltration	infiltración
infringe	ne pas respecter	infringir
inheritance tax	droit de mutation après décès	impuesto sobre sucesiones
injunction	injonction	requerimiento judicial
instigate	être l'instigateur de	instigar
intellectual property (IP)	propriété intellectuelle	propiedad intelectual
invalid	nul et non avenu	inválido
investor	actionnaire	inversor
jargon	jargon	argot
jeopardise	compromettre	arriesgar
judgment	jugement	sentencia
judge	juge	juez
judicial authority	pouvoir judiciaire	autoridad judicial

Absetzung	pisemne zeznanie pod przysięgą
Bagatellisierung	uchylenie od zasady
abschrecken, abhalten	powstrzymać, odstraszyć
diplomatischer Schutz	ochrona dyplomatyczna
ausbezahlen, ausgeben	wypłacać
Enthüllung	wyjawienie
Diskriminierung, Benachteiligung	dyskryminacja
Streit	spór
verbreiten	rozpowszechniać
Verzerrung	spaczenie, fałszywe przedstawienie
Verleiher	dystrybutorzy (filmu)
Doktrin	doktryna
wohnhaft	udomowiony
Drogenkartell	kartele narkotykowe
die im Verkehr erforderliche Sorgfalt	właściwa dbałość
ungeheuerlich	skandaliczny, jawny
veruntreute Gelder	przywłaszczone fundusze
Chancengleichheit	jednakowe możliwości
Beweismaterial	dowód, dowody
etwas seine Gültigkeit nehmen, auslöschen	wypatroszyć (w przenośni)
Fälschung	fałszywy, podróbka
Bundesgericht	sąd federalny
Verfahren einleiten	wnieść powództwo
Geldstrafe	grzywna
Franchise	franczyza
Betrug	defraudacja
Sorgerecht	przyznać prawa do opieki
Grund	podstawy, uzasadnienie
Hacker	hacker
als rechtswidrig ansehen	uznać za nielegalne, za bezprawne
hiermit	niniejszym
nachstehend, im Folgenden	po czym
falscher Alarm	oszustwo, mistyfikacja
haftbar machen	uznać kogoś odpowiedzialnym za
Holdinggesellschaft	towarzystwo holdingowe posiadające akcje innych firm
unrechtmäßige Gelder	nieuczciwie zdobyte pieniądze
illegal, rechtswidrig	nielegalny
verboten	bezprawny, nielegalny
Immunität	zwolnienie, immunitet
andeutungsweise	w sposób dorozumiany, milcząco
entschädigen	wynagradzać straty
Infiltration, Unterwanderung	infiltracja
verletzen, übertreten	naruszać
Erbschaftssteuer	podatek spadkowy
einstweilige Verfügung	nakaz sądowy, zakaz sądowy
anstiften	rozpocząć
geistiges Eigentum	własność intelektualna
ungültig	nieważny
Kapitalanleger	inwestor
Jargon, Fachsprache	żargon
gefährden	narażać na niebezpieczeństwo
Gerichtsurteil	orzeczenie, wyrok
Richter	sędzia
Gerichtsbarkeit	władza sędziowska

jurisdiction	juridiction, tribunaux compétents	jurisdicción
launder	blanchir	blanquear
lax	relâché, négligeant	relajado
legal proceedings	poursuites judiciaires	proceso
legal right or duty	droit ou obligation légales	derecho o deber legal
levy a fine	imposer une amende	imponer una multa
liberalisation	libéralisation	liberalización
licensee	concessionnaire	titular
limitation injunctive	restriction injonctive	prescripción de requerimiento judicial
litigation	litige	litigación
malice	malice, malveillance	malicia
merit	mériter	merecer
mining lease	concession minière	arrendamiento minero
misappropriation	distraction de bien	apropiación indebida
motion	motion	moción
municipality	municipalité	municipalidad
nefarious	vil	nefario
non-disclosure	non-divulgation	no divulgación
notary	notaire	notario
nullify	annuler	anular
obscure	obscur	oscuro
offshore haven	refuge extraterritorial	paraíso fiscal
online auction	enchères en ligne	subasta en línea
operating income	bénéfices d'exploitation	ingresos de explotación
overturn an agreement	annuler un accord	anular un contrato
party, parties	partie, parties	parte, partes
patent	brevet	patente
pending	en attendant l'issue de	pendiente
perception	perception	percepción
perjury	parjure, fausse allégation	perjurio
perpetrate a scam	perpétrer une escroquerie	perpetrar un fraude
place of origin	lieu d'origine	lugar de origen
plaintiff	plaignant, requérant	demandante
plant	installation industrielle	planta
practice	cabinet	bufete
precedential	ayant capacité jurisprudentielle	precedente
prefer an accusation	porter une accusation	presentar una acusación
prevail	prévaloir	prevalecer
proclaim	proclamer, déclarer que	proclamar
professional trade association	association professionnelle	asociación comercial profesional
proprietors	propriétaires	propietarios
purport	de soi-disant	supuesto
pursuant	en vertu de	de conformidad
receipt	réception	recibo
recipient	bénéficiaire	beneficiario
reckless indifference	négligence coupable	indiferencia temeraria
recourse	recours	recurrir
regime	régime	régimen
regulators	régulateurs	reguladores
resolution	résolution	resolución
retailer	détaillant	minorista
rival bid	offre concurrente	oferta rival
rule	décider, règle	disponer, disposición
safeguard	protection	protección

Zuständigkeit	jurysdykcja
waschen	prać (pieniądze)
lax	niedbały, rozwiązły, słaby, bez dyscypliny
Verfahren	postępowanie prawne
Gesetzlicher Anspruch oder Pflicht	prawo podmiotowe, obowiązek prawny
Geldstrafe erheben	nałożyć grzywnę
Liberalisierung	liberalizacja
Lizenzinhaber	licencjobiorca
Einschränkungsverfügung	nakaz ograniczający
Prozeß, Rechtsstreit	spór sądowy, proces
böse Absicht	złośliwość
Verdienst	zasługiwać na
zeitlich begrenzte Schürfrechte	dzierżawa kopalniana
Unterschlagung	przywłaszczenie
Antrag	wniosek
Stadtverwaltung	gmina miejska, zarząd miejski
ruchlos, verrucht	nikczemny, niegodziwy
Verletzung der Anzeigepflicht	nieujawnienie, zatajenie
Notar	notariusz
annullieren	unieważniać, anulować
unklar, vage	nieznany
Offshore-Hafen	raj podatkowy
Online-Auktion	aukcja on-line
Betriebseinkommen	dochody z eksploatacji
Abkommen aufheben	obalić umowę
Partei, Parteien	strona, strony
Patent	patent
schwebend	w toku
Wahrnehmung, Auffassung	percepcja
Meineid	krzywoprzysięstwo
Betrug begehen	popełnić przestępstwo
Ursprungsort	miejsce pochodzenia
Kläger	powód, strona skarżąca
Produktionsanlage	fabryka, zakład
Praxis	kancelaria
Präzedenzfall	precedensowy
anklagen	wnosić oskarżenie
sich durchsetzen	uzyskać przewagę, przeważać
erklären	obwieszczać, wprowadzać ograniczenia
professionelle Handelsvereinigung	profesjonalna organizacja handlowa
Inhaber	właściciele
angeblich etwas tun	rzekomy
gemäß	zgodny z czymś
Erhalt	odbiór
Empfänger	odbiorca
grob Fahrlässigkeit	lekkomyślna obojętność
Inanspruchnahme	uciekanie się do czegoś
Regelung	reżim
aufsichtführende Personen	regulatorzy
Resolution, Beschluß	rozwiązanie
Einzelhändler	handlowiec
Übernahmeangebot	konkurująca oferta
beurteilen	wydać postanowienie, postanowić; reguła
schützen	zabezpieczenie, ochrona

securities	valeurs	valores
seek redress	demander réparation	rectificar
seizure warrants	mandats de saisie	órdenes de embargo
set forth	exposer	consignar
shell company	société fictive	sociedad ficticia
signatory	signataire	signatario
siphon off	canaliser	desviar
solicitor	« solicitor »	abogado
standard clause	clause type	cláusula tipo
standing instruction	directives	reglamento general
statutory obligation	obligation légale	obligación legal
stay proceedings	suspension d'instance	sobreseer
stock manipulation	tripotage de valeurs	manipulación de acciones
subject to	sous réserve de	sujeto a
submit to	soumis à	someter a
subsisting	subsistant	existente
suit, lawsuit	procès	pleito
tax rate	taux de l'impôt	tasa impositiva
tender	offre	ofrecer
terminate	mettre fin à	terminar
thereafter	après cela, par la suite	posteriormente
thereof	des présentes	de la misma
tissue	tissu	tejido
tort	préjudice	agravio
trademark	marque de fabrique	marca registrada
traffic rights	droits d'exploitation	derechos de comercio
treaty	traité	tratado
trial	(faire passer en) jugement	juicio
turnover	rendement	facturación
umpire	surarbitre	árbitro
unauthorised	non-autorisé	no autorizado
unclaimed land	terrain non revendiqué	terreno sin reclamar
under licence	sous licence	bajo licencia
undertaking	entreprise commerciale	compromiso
unmask	démasquer	desenmascarar
unwary	trop confiant	ingenuo
uphold a decision	maintenir une décision	confirmar una decisión
verdict	verdict	veredicto
violate a law	enfreindre une loi	violar una ley
waive	renoncer	eximir
warranty	garantie	garantía
watchdog	observateur officiel	controlador
whereas	attendu que	por cuanto
wholesaler	grossiste	mayorista
will	testament	testamento

Wertpapiere	papiery wartościowe
Wiedergutmachung verlangen	starać się o odszkodowanie
Pfändungsbescheid	nakaz zajęcia, konfiskata
darlegen	oświadczać, przedstawiać, wyjaśniać, przedkładać
Scheinfirmen	przedsiębiorstwo fikcyjne
Unterzeichner	sygnatariusz
abziehen, abschöpfen	odciągać (np. fundusze, aktywa)
Rechtsanwalt	adwokat nie występujący w sądach, radca prawny
Standardklausel	standardowa klauzula
bestehende Anordnung	stale obowiązujące instrukcje, stałe polecenie/zlecenie
gesetzliche Verpflichtung	przymus prawny, ustawowe zobowiązanie
ein Verfahren zeitweise einstellen	zawieszać postępowanie w sprawie
Aktienmanipulierung	manipulacje na rynku akcji, manipulowanie akcjami
vorbehaltlich, abhängig von	pod warunkiem, z zastrzeżeniem
sich unterwerfen	przedłożyć (komuś)
bestehend aus	utrzymujący się
Klage	pozew sądowy, proces, powództwo
Steuersatz	stopa podatkowa
anbieten	oferować
beenden	zakończyć, rozwiązać (umowę)
danach, darauf	poniżej
davon	tego, jego (o wymienionym podmiocie)
Gewebe	tkanka
unerlaubte Handlung	delikt, czyn niedozwolony
Warenzeichen	znak handlowy
Verkehrsrecht	prawa przewozowe
Abkommen	traktat, układ, umowa
Gerichtsverhandlung	rozprawa sądowa
Umsatz	obrót, obieg, płynność (kadr)
Schiedsrichter	sędzia polubowny, arbiter, rozjemca
unbefugt, unberechtigt	nie upoważniony, niedozwolony, bezprawny
herrenloser Boden	grunty/nieruchomości do których nikt nie zgłosił praw
mit Lizenzgenehmigung	z upoważnienia, za zezwoleniem, na licencji
Unternehmung	przedsięwzięcie, podjęcie się
entlarven	zdemaskować
unbesonnen	nieostrożny, nierozważny
ein Urteil bestätigen	popierać decyzję
Urteil	wyrok
gegen ein Gesetz verstoßen	naruszyć prawo
verzichten auf	zrzec się
Garantie	gwarancja
Kontrollorgan	jednostka nadzorująca
während	skoro, jednakże
Großhändler	hurtownik
Testament	testament, wola

Key

Reading tasks

A 1 There may be bias or unfair advantages in the home country of the business partner.
  2 Shipping, commodities and construction.
  3 Three arbitrators, one chosen by each party and the third, the chairman, selected by both parties.
  4 Arbitration takes place in private, litigation takes place in court.
  5 Paris, London, Geneva, Stockholm, New York, Hong Kong and Singapore.
  6 Stockholm.
  7 Activities and rules.
  8 Speed, cost effectiveness, confidentiality and reliability of the arbitrators and their decisions.
  9 Accountants and engineers.
 10 No.

B 2 T   3 T   4 T   5 T   6 T   7 T   8 F

Vocabulary tasks

A 2 h   3 e   4 f   5 a   6 k   7 i   8 b   9 g   10 c   11 l   12 j

B 2 arbitrator   3 arbitration   4 delaying tactics   5 settle   6 dispute
  7 arbitrate   8 disagree   9 resolution   10 agree

C 2 plaintiff/defendant   3 buyer/seller   4 borrower/lender
  5 wholesaler/retailers   6 lawyer/client   7 licensee/licensor
  8 franchiser/franchisees   9 undersigned   10 parties to the agreement

D 2 arbitration   3 licensor/licensee   4 licence   5 franchise   6 franchiser/franchisee

Reading tasks

A 1 Employment discrimination.
  2 In the US Supreme Court.
  3 Ms Kolstad.
  4 Sex, race, age and other types of employment discrimination.
  5 She suffered sex discrimination at work.
  6 No.
  7 The court dismissed the appeal for punitive damages.
  8 The US Chamber of Commerce.
  9 Between $50,000 and $300,000.

B 2 b   3 c   4 b   5 b   6 a

Vocabulary tasks

A 2 circuit judge   3 Act   4 cap   5 jury   6 federal rights
  7 punitive damages   8 egregious   9 appeal   10 settlement   11 lawsuit   12 brief

B 2 f   3 a   4 h   5 i   6 b   7 g   8 d   9 j   10 e

C 2 under   3 on   4 on   5 to   6 at, on   7 to against   8 to

D 2 On the other hand   3 Conversely   4 If   5 whereas   6 Should, might

Reading tasks

A 2 F   3 F   4 T   5 F

B 1 The European Commission.
  2 Member states created serious competition distortions by unilaterally granting US carriers rights while ensuring exclusivity for their own carriers.
  3 It wants an EU-wide policy.
  4 BA hopes to get a full alliance with American Airlines.
  5 The Commissioner checks that EU countries do not distort competition.
  6 During the transition towards full liberalisation.

C 2 BA.
4 The European Transport Commission.
6 The European Transport Commission.
3 Deals between European and US carriers.
5 The eight European countries.

Vocabulary tasks

A 1 a   **2** a   **3** c   **4** b   **5** c   **6** b

B 2 f   **3** d   **4** a   **5** h   **6** e   **7** g   **8** c

C 2 competition   **3** unfair competition   **4** regulated   **5** deregulated
   6 Free trade   **7** protectionism   **8** regulation

Unit 4 Reading tasks

A 1 Its distinctive character and its reputation.
  2 Article 177 of the EC Treaty re: Article 4(1)b of the Directive of 21 December 1988.
  3 MGM produces video film cassettes and film distribution and projection for cinemas and television. Canon Kabushiki Kaisha produce's still and motion picture cameras and projectors, television filming, recording, transmission, receiving and reproduction devices.
  4 They believed it infringed their world trademark.
  5 The Japanese company.
  6 It considered whether the distinctive character of the trademark and its reputation should be taken into account, and whether there was likely to be confusion about places of origin.
  7 It guarantees the identity of the origin of the product.
  8 Mistaking one brand for another.
  9 Fair (undistorted) competition.
 10 MGM was not able to register its *Cannon* trademark in Germany. Canon Kabushiki Kaisha won the case.

B 1 Because the trademark's reputation must be protected from other similar trademarks which could 'borrow' the brand or associations that belong to it.
  2 It is established in the market and the public identifies it as possessing certain qualities.
  3 The public may be confused about which company makes the product on sale. The trademark should clearly belong to only one company.
  4 Because companies work hard to make their trademarks immediately recognisable. The image, picture or logo help the public identify the origin of the product.
  5 It means that one company is responsible for all the goods or services carrying their trademark.
  6 Yes.
  7 No. (*distorted* means unfair)
  8 In commercial competition between very similar products the reputation of quality carried by a trademark may influence the customer's buying decision.

Vocabulary tasks

A 2 e   **3** d   **4** g   **5** f   **6** a   **7** c

B 2 take into account   **3** course of proceedings   **4** goods or services   **5** likelihood of confusion

C 2 led him to think   **3** copy   **4** impersonate

D 2 according to case law   **3** within the meaning of   **4** proper construction
  5 It was held   **6** for the purpose of

E 2 in, of   **3** on, of   **4** in, by   **5** with, to
  6 of, in, for, under   **7** Within, to, of   **8** under, of

Unit 5 Reading tasks

A 2 F   **3** F   **4** F   **5** T   **6** T

B 1 The recommendation to allow human cloning for spare parts and a proposed merger between two large pharmaceutical companies.
  2 Two. (UK Human Fertilisation and Embryology Authority; European Commission Biotechnology Directive).
  3 They need to produce a complete set of contractual documentation.
  4 A wake up call; the companies are alerted to the fact that there is a problem.

5 Ethical debates about whether it is morally right to make money out of medical advances.
6 They might copy and patent the discoveries themselves.
7 Scratch the surface.
8 It causes complex and puzzling issues.

Vocabulary tasks

A 2 j 3 f 4 g 5 h 6 b 7 i 8 a 9 e 10 d

B 2 scratch the surface 3 gone up in smoke 4 avalanche of complaints 5 a landmark case
6 stop the leak 7 cast a shadow over 8 plug the gap 9 dawned on

C 2 g 3 f 4 a 5 d 6 e 7 h 8 b

D 2 trickle 3 cascade 4 stream 5 torrents 6 flood

E 1 c 2 a 3 d 4 e 5 b

Unit 6

Reading tasks (Reading 1)

A 1 Aboriginal groups and environmentalists.
2 They are trying to stop a uranium mine being developed in Jabiluka.
3 The Mirrar Aboriginal people.
4 Twenty years.
5 The High Court.
6 The 1976 Land Rights Act gave them custody of the land.
7 No.
8 North, a diversified mining company.
9 A situation where neither party can gain an advantage, so neither of them does anything.
10 On time, according to the company's plans.

B 2 F 3 T 4 F 5 T 6 F 7 F 8 T

Vocabulary tasks

A 2 overturned 3 block 4 stand-off 5 stand in the way of 6 held up

B 2 ruling 3 regulation 4 regulated/regulatory 5 judge
6 judicious 7 decision 8 decisive 9 approve
10 approved/approving 11 permission 12 permitted

Reading tasks (Reading 2)

A 1 Yes. 4 Diamonds.
2 Almost two years before the article was written. 5 The territorial government and four native groups.
3 Northwest Canada.

B 1 North. 6 low, high
2 Tribal. 7 uranium, diamonds
3 privately owned 8 Canadian mine, Australian mine
4 Received government support after discussion. 9 Canada, Australia
5 Profitable. 10 Canada, Australia

Unit 7

Reading tasks

A 1 Confidentiality Undertaking.
2 Two: Target (the company) and Princeton Limited.
3 Read and sign the letter.
4 Three: Confidential Information, Representatives, Relevant Material.
5 Evaluating, negotiating, advising on or implementing a proposed transaction.
6 Princeton must notify Target Enterprises in writing.
7 Two years.
8 By a written document executed by Target Enterprises and Princeton.

B 1 Target Enterprises is giving the confidential information.
2 Disclose confidential information to third parties.
3 Princeton Limited.
4 1c

5 1e
6 2a–d
7 Yes (clause 2a)
8 Yes (clause 2b)
9 Court of competent jurisdiction, any government department, any recognised stock exchange agency or any other regulatory body.
10 Two: both Target Enterprises and Princeton Limited.

Vocabulary tasks

A **2** h   **3** l   **4** e   **5** d   **6** j   **7** a   **8** c   **9** g   **10** f
B **2** f   **3** g   **4** h   **5** j   **6** d   **7** e   **8** c   **9** a   **10** l

C **2** hereinafter   **3** herewith   **4** therefore   **5** hereto

D **2** will (When will you be back this evening?)
    3 shall (This document doesn't give the company any rights)
    4 shall (The company will destroy all materials if asked)
    5 will (If you carry the boxes, I'll carry the bags)
    6 shall (Princeton isn't responsible for what the information says)
    7 will (What do you think he'll say when …)
    8 shall (The company won't mention the materials without permission)

Unit 8

Reading tasks

A **1** A licensed edition of a paperback book.
    2 The agreement comes into effect when the advance payment has been made.
    3 No, not without written permission being obtained in advance from the Proprietors.
    4 In clause 5 the Proprietors guarantee that there will be no legal problems with copyright and agree to compensate the Publishers if they incur any loss, injury or expense as a result of such problems.
    5 The Publisher must get the Proprietors' consent in writing beforehand.
    6 No.
    7 They will go to arbitration.
    8 They will take the matter to an English court.

B **1** Yes. It is mentioned in clause 2.
    2 The Publishers, the book.
    3 The warranty that assures the Publishers about copyright.
    4 'Rights' are the things the parties are entitled to under the agreement; 'liabilities' are the things they are obliged to do by the agreement.
    5 Any difference between the two parties.
    6 An umpire is someone involved in the arbitration who makes sure that both parties obey the rules.
    7 No.
    8 *Statutory modification, re-enactment.*

Vocabulary tasks

A **2** e   **3** f   **4** a   **5** d   **6** n   **7** b   **8** o
    9 g   **10** m   **11** k   **12** j   **13** i   **14** h   **15** l

B **2** hereinafter termed, hereinafter termed   **5** prior written consent   **8** revert to
    3 come into effect   **6** touching the meaning
    4 exclusive   **7** Subject to

C **2** detailed   **3** in no way whatever   **4** indemnify   **5** extended to include

Unit 9

Reading tasks

A **1** 71m ounces.
    2 C$6bn.
    3 Toronto and Texas.
    4 About 2,000.
    5 The company (Bre-X Minerals), its directors and the brokerage firms who recommended the company to investors.
    6 They could be liable every time the information they give to investors turns out to be incorrect.

7 Yes.

8 Bre-X, its engineering firms and brokerages and Barrick.

9 Barrick is accused of giving out false information about Bre-X and hiding information that showed that Bre-X was a bad investment.

10 It is bankrupt.

B 1 Reported mining results.

2 The gold find could make Bre-X one of the world's biggest mining companies.

3 He died falling out of a helicopter.

4 They lost one third of their value.

5 It was overloaded by heavy trading in Bre-X shares.

6 Ontario Securities regulators.

7 An independent audit showed no gold at Busang.

Vocabulary tasks

A	**2** h	**3** e	**4** i	**5** j	**6** g	**7** c	**8** d	**9** f	**10** a
B	**2** g	**3** d	**4** e	**5** a	**6** c	**7** j	**8** i	**9** f	**10** h

C 2 brokerages   **4** participated ... fraud ... market   **6** securities
3 small investors   **5** aiders ... abettors

Unit 10   Reading tasks

A 1 The telephone company.

2 It is a part of BT that issues calling cards.

3 £200m.

4 About 110,000.

5 It is mainly organised by professional criminals.

6 Opening an account in a false name, selling calls and disappearing when the bill arrives.

7 By using new technology like Sheriff to detect and prove fraud.

8 By using artificial intelligence to detect frauds and share the information across product lines.

B 1 The cost in dollars to telephone operators in lost revenue.

2 The number of reported fraudulent phone calls.

3 The number of fraudulent calls to Sri Lanka sold by a Tamil group.

4 The cost of the 400,000 fraudulent calls sold by a Tamil group.

5 The minimum number of calls Sheriff sorts per day.

C 2 false   **3** make   **4** pay   **5** distance   **6** due

Vocabulary tasks

A 2 BT's   **3** the system   **4** telephone fraud
5 notorious individuals   **6** a gang of Tamil sympathisers   **7** the system   **8** BT's

B 2 doubled the number of frauds spotted   **5** put the gang on trial
3 big time crime   **6** advanced 'object-orientated' database
4 disappearing when the bill is due   **7** tailored

C 1 prove   **4** arrested, convicted, imprisoned
2 fraud, barons of organised crime   **5** false name
3 evidence

D 2 a   **3** e   **4** d   **5** b

E *People:* assault, rape, kidnapping, bribery, blackmail
Others: robbery, fraud, forgery, perjury, burglary, money laundering

Unit 11   Reading tasks

A 1 Las Vegas.

2 106 (22 + 14 + 70)

3 Break up the money laundering gangs in Mexico.

4 $200bn.

5 $500bn.

6 A quarter of 1%.

7 New electronic banking technology, the globalisation of finance and speed of operation of the international banking system have made it easier. The systems used are cash-less transactions, electronic trading and computerised clearing.

8 Yes.

9 By using offshore financial havens where regulation is not strict; by exploiting banking secrecy; by setting up shell companies; by setting up offshore trusts where the authorities don't ask awkward questions; by using 'walking accounts'.

10 Commercial confidentiality, legal tax avoidance, capital transfers at low or nil tax rates and disguising corporate ownership.

B 1 Money which is moved around by computer – cashless transactions, electronic trading and computerised clearing.

2 Settlement or loans.

3 So they can catch criminals when they are depositing cash.

4 The people who own the accounts or earn money from them.

5 An account that can be easily moved at the first sign of any official enquiries.

6 They can be set up quickly and easily with minimum investigation.

7 A basic level of funds. (the amount they have to have varies from place to place)

8 In large amounts of cash in high denomination bills, often under diplomatic cover. (carried in the diplomatic bags used by embassies which are not searched at customs)

9 They will convert cash into gambling chips then change the chips back into cash again.

10 Some offer immediate electronic transfer to an offshore bank account.

Vocabulary tasks

A 2 warrants 3 final 4 estimate 5 money 6 trading 7 exposure
8 financial 9 commercial 10 capital 11 offshore 12 chips

B 2 commercial confidentiality 3 risk exposure 4 seizure warrants
5 capital transfers 6 electronic trading 7 financial havens
8 offshore financial centres 9 conservative estimate 10 final version
11 ill-gotten money 12 gambling chips

C 2 lure 3 alleged 4 recover 5 damage 6 gloomy 7 spot
8 disguise 9 illicit 10 gambling

Unit 12 Reading tasks

A 1 Stock manipulations, pyramid scams, Ponzi schemes.

2 The online world.

3 Commercial bulletin boards, live discussion groups (chats), e-mail, information web pages.

4 They can operate and disappear easily; no one can see them or identify them.

5 National Consumer League, Internet Fraud Watch.

6 Online auction fraud.

7 Yes.

8 Internet Fraud Watch.

9 Escrow services hold the money in a special account until the buyer has received the goods in satisfactory condition. They then release it to the seller.

B 1 Through online services accessed on computers and the Internet.

2 By so-called experts sending out false information about listed companies.

3 Frauds involving: web auctions; the sale of general merchandise; Internet services; hardware or software; business opportunities such as pyramid schemes.

4 True.

5 No.

C b) 8 c) 6 d) 5 e) 7 f) 9 g) 10 h) 2 i) 4 j) 1

Vocabulary tasks

A 1 c 2 c 3 b 4 a 5 c 6 b 7 a 8 c

B 2 rulings 3 redress 4 fraudulent
5 liable 6 fines 7 counterfeiting
8 misrepresentation 9 faulty 10 false

C 2 credit card, by cheque   3 offline payments   4 Money up-front
    5 money order   6 escrow fund   7 advance loan fees

Unit 13

Before you read
2 2 d   3 g   4 f   5 h   6 c   7 j   8 a   9 e   10 i

Reading tasks
A 2 T   3 T   4 T   5 F   6 T   7 F   8 T

Vocabulary tasks
A 2 substantial revenues   3 ancillary   4 accrue
    5 arbitrated amount   6 compensation   7 bonus clause
    8 deposition   9 deficits   10 plaintiff
B 2 h   3 i   4 j   5 f   6 e   7 a   8 c   9 d   10 g
C 2 drew up   3 renew   4 signed   5 bid for   6 broken   7 void   8 exchange

Unit 14

Reading tasks
A 1 Drugs/pharmaceuticals.
   2 Yes.
   3 The SEC was worried that over-optimistic press reports on the success of the company's new drug had misled investors over the true value of the company's shares.
   4 Increased.
   5 Head of clinical research.
   6 He had revealed confidential information to third parties.

B 2 British Biotech's   3 press interest   4 the new drugs under trial
    5 the main investors in Biotech   6 Dr Millar's actions   7 British Biotech

Vocabulary tasks
A 2 sacked   6 causing serious side-effects
    3 following extensive media coverage   7 negative assessments
    4 campaign to oust the chief executive   8 fired without compensation
    5 achieve regulatory approval
B 2 g   3 f   4 d   5 a   6 e   7 b

Unit 15

Before you read
2 g   3 f   4 d   5 b   6 h   7 j
8 i   9 a   10 e

Reading tasks
A 2 Brambi Fruits.
   3 Three. (the Australian exporter which issued the bill of lading, the Dutch company which carried the fruit, and the master of the ship)
   4 Australian.
   5 They ripened prematurely because the ship's cooling system broke down.
   6 No.
   7 The bill of lading did not constitute a contract between the Dutch parties and Brambi Fruits.
B 2 f   3 g   4 e   5 h   6 a   7 c

Vocabulary tasks
A 2 damaged consignment   3 breach of contract   4 bill of lading
    5 declined jurisdiction   6 confirmed that decision   7 stayed proceedings
    8 pending   9 enforcement   10 commercial judgements
B 2 a   3 g   4 c   5 e   6 f   7 h   8 a

Unit 16

Reading tasks

A 1 The victims of a factory fire and their personal representatives.
2 At the Imperial Foods Products chicken-processing factory in the town of Hamlet, North Carolina.
3 The State of North Carolina.
4 The Tort Claims Act.
5 The exits were unmarked, blocked or inaccessible.
6 83.
7 Yes.

B 1 b   **2** b   **3** b   **4** b   **5** a   **6** b

Vocabulary tasks

A 2 a   **3** d   **4** e   **5** c   **6** h   **7** i   **8** g   **9** f   **10** k
11 m   **12** j   **13** k   **14** q   **15** o   **16** n   **17** p

B 1 *Agree:* share the opinion, affirm, adopt the decision, treat as true, assent.
Disagree: dismiss the motion, reverse a decision, dismiss claims, dissent.
2 *Agree to differ:* the parties still disagree but have decided to accept the situation rather than continue trying to persuade each other to change opinions.

C 2 share the opinion   **3** reversed the decision   **4** adopted, affirmed
5 dismiss, claims   **6** assent

D 2 e   **3** d   **4** a   **5** c   **6** f

Unit 17

Reading tasks

A 2 T   **3** T   **4** F   **5** T   **6** T   **7** T   **8** T   **9** T   **10** F   **11** T   **12** T
B 1 a   **2** c   **3** a   **4** c   **5** b   **6** c   **7** b   **8** b   **9** c   **10** b

C 1 barrister, attorney-at-law   **2** prosecutor, Crown Prosecutor
3 Queen's Counsellor, judicial school, two

Vocabulary tasks

A 2 h   **3** j   **4** i   **5** g   **6** f   **7** e   **8** d   **9** a   **10** c

B 1 instigate a prosecution   **2** bring a case   **3** infringed my copyright
4 settle out of court   **5** charge a fee   **6** reach a verdict
7 defend their clients   **8** preparing briefs   **9** arrest the suspect

C 2 c   **3** g   **4** j   **5** i   **6** e   **7** f   **8** a   **9** h   **10** d

Unit 18

Reading tasks

A 1 Kjeld Kirk Kristiansen.
2 It will have to pay a very large sum of money in inheritance tax.
3 It is defined as a finance company.
4 No.
5 Sweden.
6 The law has changed so that an inheritor has to pay tax on the capital value of a company based in a foreign country.
7 The money would be used for investment in the company and jobs.
8 Not at all.

B 1 Recently.   **4** No.   **7** Yes, so far.
2 To keep Lego family-owned.   **5** Tax-to-GDP.   **8** Smaller.
3 Foreigners.   **6** DKr3bn ($437m).

Vocabulary tasks

A 2 inherit   **3** inheritance tax   **4** company   **5** domiciled   **6** corporate
7 holding   **8** inheritor   **9** capital   **10** shares

B 2 a   **3** e   **4** f   **5** h   **6** g   **7** d   **8** c

C 2 on   **3** up   **4** by   **5** into   **6** down, to   **7** over
8 for, for   **9** to, of   **10** about

D 2 i   **3** a   **4** h   **5** d   **6** e   **7** f   **8** j   **9** g   **10** c

Check Test 1 (Units 1–9)

A Complete the sentences with the correct word. The first letter of the word is given.

1 Something which is very important is c.................... .

2 In law abiding countries, all citizens have r.................... to justice.

3 Coffee, gold and precious metals are all c.................... .

4 The right place to discuss important issues is a f ....

5 When you promise to keep something a secret you are promising to respect c.................... .

6 Good employers promise men and women e.................... at work.

7 Another word for *agreements* is s.................... .

8 When two parties agree to do something, the agreement is b.................... .

9 Changing the intended meaning of a law slightly is to d.................... it.

10 If you buy shares in a company you are an i.................... .

11 A new discovery must be protected by a p.................... .

12 Fashion-conscious people like to wear clothes that have famous b....................
   n.................... .

13 Companies can register t.................... which then only they may use.

14 When two companies decide to join together, it is called a m.................... .

15 Inaccurate and false information may be described as m.................... .

B Choose the best answer: **a**, **b**, **c** or **d**.

1 Someone who assists others to reach an agreement after a dispute is an ....
   a) aide   **b)** accomplice   **c)** arbitrator   **d)** assistant

2 She was .... of stealing documents from the office.
   a) discovered   **b)** accused   **c)** charged   **d)** found

3 Both parties in the civil case agreed to .... out of court.
   a) sue   **b)** sign   **c)** settle   **d)** submit

4 People who sign a contract are know as .... to the agreement.
   a) parties   **b)** signers   **c)** partials   **d)** signatures

5 Name .... is important to establish a centre for arbitration.
   a) recognition   **b)** dropping   **c)** changes   **d)** awareness

6 A famous name may not be used by anyone else if it has been registered – a world trademark must not be ....
   a) hijacked   **b)** appeared   **c)** directed   **d)** infringed

7 The technical name in English law for legal disputes that go to court is ....
   a) legal match   **b)** court scene   **c)** attack   **d)** litigation

8 The factory near my house makes fashion clothing under ....
   a) licence   **b)** invention   **c)** claimant   **d)** citation

9 A .... is the owner of a business such as a shop or restaurant.

   a) private   **b)** peer   **c)** proprietor   **d)** parson

10 The contract states the licensee is not allowed to .... or change anything.

   a) swap   **b)** intervene   **c)** appendix   **d)** abridge

11 The person who brings a complaint in a civil case is called the ....

   a) petitioner   **b)** plaintiff   **c)** complainer   **d)** civilian

12 Someone who shows .... does not act fairly and treats one party preferentially.

   a) deception   **b)** bias   **c)** perjury   **d)** treachery

13 .... damages are designed to deter others from committing the same crime.

   a) punishment   **b)** compensation   **c)** capital   **d)** punitive

14 A jury will bring in .... of guilty when there is no reasonable doubt.

   a) a verdict   **b)** a decree   **c)** a decision   **d)** an edict

15 When someone goes to court in a civil matter, they file a ....

   a) suiting   **b)** pursuance   **c)** pursuit   **d)** suit

16 The decision will have a serious .... effect for the whole industry.

   a) side   **b)** impact   **c)** knock-on   **d)** damage

17 When someone suffers .... they are treated unfairly due to gender or colour.

   a) assault   **b)** ambush   **c)** discrimination   **d)** derogation

18 In US legal terms, showing disgraceful disrespect is called .... behaviour.

   a) contemptuous   **b)** discourteous   **c)** egregious   **d)** discounted

19 A .... ruling is not the final decision of the court.

   a) partial   **b)** purposeful   **c)** preliminary   **d)** particular

20 The fear of going to prison .... potential criminals from committing crimes.

   a) deters   **b)** defers   **c)** incites   **d)** distracts

21 The .... sentences the defendant after the jurors have brought in a guilty verdict.

   a) jurist   **b)** jury   **c)** foreman   **d)** judge

22 The legal processes of taking someone to court is called a ....

   a) lawyer   **b)** lawsuit   **c)** jurisdiction   **d)** litigant

23 The solicitor prepared a .... for the barrister.

   a) brief   **b)** trap   **c)** breeze   **d)** briefcase

24 That is an exception – it is not the ....

   a) normal   **b)** normality   **c)** norm   **d)** nominal

25 When farmers get permission to use someone's land, they are granted a ....

   a) letting   **b)** lease   **c)** licence   **d)** landmark

Check Test 2 (Units 10–18)

A Complete the sentence with the correct word. The first letter of the word is given.

1 Only with the c.................. of the bank employees could the criminal launder his money.

2 They d.................. their appearance so that no one would recognise them.

3 Another word for illegal and wrong is i.................. .

4 Selling and promoting goods over the phone is called t.................. .

5 Let me give you some practical advice and some helpful t.................. on how to succeed.

6 The business was very successful – it was a f.................. concern.

7 Fraudulent schemes are often called s.................. .

8 Traditional, non-electronic payments are made o.................. .

9 When you open a bank account, you may be asked to show your passport or birth certificate as v.................. that you are who you say you are.

10 The result was c.................. on the agreement and cooperation of the others.

11 The normal c.................. arrangements will apply: both parties must sign, with a witness.

12 As a reward for your excellent trading results, you have been awarded a b.................. .

13 Very technical vocabulary used by experts is known as j.................. .

14 All the a.................. of the company must appear on the balance sheet.

15 A written statement of evidence given by a witness is called a d.................. .

B Choose the best answer: **a**, **b**, **c** or **d**.

1 When you are legally responsible for something, you are said to be ....
   a) lawful   **b)** legal   **c)** leasehold   **d)** liable

2 The robber tried to terrify the shopkeeper by threatening him with a .... gun.
   a) false   **b)** forged   **c)** fraud   **d)** fake

3 It looked like my signature on the cheque but it was not – someone had .... it.
   a) forged   **b)** cheated   **c)** framed   **d)** reproduced

4 The authorities found that she had given them a .... name and address.
   a) forged   **b)** false   **c)** infamous   **d)** fraud

5 Working in the accounts department gave her a wonderful opportunity to .... the company of thousands of pounds.
   a) defraud   **b)** embarrass   **c)** embrace   **d)** embroil

6 Did you say he could borrow the car? Or did he just take it without your ....
   a) consort   **b)** consent   **c)** know-how   **d)** service

7 In Great Britain, you are assumed to be innocent until shown by a court otherwise – the prosecution has to prove your ....
   a) charge   **b)** accusation   **c)** guile   **d)** guilt

8 When she lost her credit card, the first thing she did was to call the bank and .... it.
   a) confess   **b)** condemn   **c)** cancel   **d)** conceal

9 The penalties for causing environmental .... are considered by some to be too lenient.

a) breakdown   b) spoilage   c) depravity   d) pollution

10 Wrongs done against people or property in civil law are called ....

a) torture   b) torts   c) litigants   d) plaints

11 A QC is a lawyer in the UK who may speak in the High Court. QC stands for ....

a) Queen's Courtier   b) Queen's Consort   c) Queen's Counsellor   d) Queen's Council

12 The Lord Chancellor is responsible for the appointment of .... in the UK.

a) justice   b) juries   c) wigs   d) judges

13 She was the main .... of the rich man's will and received most of the estate.

a) beneficiary   b) benefited   c) testament   d) benefactor

14 The scientist was able to betray secrets to another country and so committed ....

a) treason   b) trickery   c) perjury   d) forgery

15 The drug dealers .... their money from one bank account to another in an attempt to conceal where it had come from.

a) took   b) transferred   c) withdrew   d) deposited

16 .... is the part of the legal profession having the right of audience in court.

a) Arbitration   b) Accounting   c) Advocacy   d) Assessing

17 The most powerful criminals are sometimes known as the .... of organised crime.

a) baronets   b) warlords   c) barons   d) gangs

18 Signing someone else's name is a .... act.

a) fraudulent   b) fraud   c) defrauded   d) forgery

19 Criminals, gangsters and mobsters are all ....

a) villains   b) villagers   c) vassals   d) victims

20 Being famous for something bad is being ....

a) known   b) unknown   c) noted   d) notorious

21 After being convicted of a serious crime, a criminal is ....

a) prosecuted   b) imposed   c) imprisoned   d) confiscated

22 Samples of blood, items of clothing and written documents are all forms of ....

a) examples   b) deposition   c) affidavits   d) evidence

23 Like clothing, money that needs to be 'cleaned up' is subject to ....

a) soaking   b) laundering   c) pressing   d) rinsing

24 The detectives operated secretly as gang members – they worked ....

a) underground   b) underage   c) undercover   d) underpaid

25 The police issued .... for their arrest.

a) warrants   b) guarantees   c) warnings   d) instructions

Check Test Key

A **1** crucial **2** recourse **3** commodities **4** forum

5 confidentiality **6** equality **7** settlements **8** bilateral

9 distort **10** investor **11** patent **12** brand names

13 trademarks **14** merger **15** misleading

B **1** c **2** b **3** c **4** a

5 a **6** d **7** d **8** a

9 c **10** d **11** b **12** b

13 d **14** a **15** d **16** c

17 c **18** c **19** c **20** a

21 d **22** b **23** a **24** c

25 b

A **1** complicity **2** disguised **3** illicit **4** telemarketing

5 tips **6** flourishing **7** scams **8** offline

9 verification **10** contingent **11** contractual **12** bonus

13 jargon **14** assets **15** deposition

B **1** d **2** d **3** a **4** b

5 a **6** b **7** d **8** c

9 d **10** b **11** c **12** d

13 a **14** a **15** b **16** c

17 c **18** a **19** a **20** d

21 c **22** d **23** c **24** d

25 a